MIRACULOUS MILESTONES
IN SCIENCE, MEDICINE &
INNOVATION
- And the Faith of
Those Who Achieved Them

∾

WILLIAM J. FEDERER

MIRACULOUS MILESTONES IN SCIENCE, MEDICINE & INNOVATION
- And the Faith of Those Who Achieved Them
by William J. Federer

For other, contact: Amerisearch, Inc.
www.AmericanMinute.com wjfederer@gmail.com
1-888-USA-WORD

Special thanks is given to Susie Federer for her invaluable inspiration and assistance in creative design and editing.

HISTORY/RELIGIOUS/EDUCATION
ISBN: 978-0-9896491-9-3

Cover design by Dustin Myers, longitudebranding.com

Amerisearch, Inc., PO Box 60442, Fort Myers, FL 33906
1-888-USA-WORD
www.AmericanMinute.com, smfederer@gmail.com

*"I observe the laws of nature ...
There are not laws without a lawgiver"*
– Albert Einstein

❧

"This most beautiful system of the sun, planets, and comets, could only proceed from the counsel and dominion of an intelligent and powerful Being … Order and life in the universe could happen only by the willful reasoning of its original Creator, whom I call the 'Lord God.'"
– Sir Isaac Newton, *Principia*, 1687

❧

"He builds his lofty palace in the heavens and sets its foundation on the earth … the Lord is his name."
– Amos 9:6

CONTENTS

INTRODUCTION

Astronomer Johannes Kepler, known for discovering laws of planetary motion, wrote in his book *The Harmonies of the World,* 1619:

> O, Almighty God, I am thinking Thy thoughts after Thee!

In 1976, Wernher von Braun, "Father of Modern Space Flight," wrote the forward to a science book, stating:

> When Astronaut Frank Borman returned from his unforgettable Christmas, 1968, flight around the moon with Apollo 8, he was told that a Soviet Cosmonaut recently returned from a space flight had commented that he had seen neither God nor angels on his flight.
>
> Had Borman seen God? the reporter inquired. Frank Borman replied, "No, I did not see Him either, but I saw His evidence."

Hopefully, as you read through this small volume, you too may see His evidence.

CR

"THE HEAVENS DECLARE THE GLORY OF GOD"

Among the eight planets, dwarf planets and other small bodies in our Solar System, the Earth is the third planet from the Sun, 93 million miles away. With light traveling at 186,000 miles per second, it takes 8.3 minutes for light to travel from the Sun to the Earth. In a year, light travels 5.88 trillion miles. The distance from our Sun to the next closest star, Proxima Centauri, is 4.3 light years.

Over 20,000 light years away is the largest star in the Milky Way Galaxy, Stephenson 2-18. It is a supergiant 2,150 times larger than the Sun. If placed in our solar system, it would engulf the orbit of Saturn, the sixth planet.

The Milky Way Galaxy has an estimated 500 billion stars. The next closest galaxy is 2.5 million light years away – the Andromeda Galaxy. It contains 1 trillion stars. The Milky Way, Andromeda, and Triangulum Galaxies, with 80 dwarf galaxies, form a cluster of galaxies called the Local Group, named by astronomer Edwin Hubble.

The Local Group is located within a larger group of galaxies – the Virgo Supercluster, which is located within an even larger group – the Laniakea Supercluster.

There are over 10 million superclusters, containing over 2 trillion galaxies, in the observable universe, which is postulated to be 93 billion light years across and expanding faster than the speed of light.

To get an idea of the immense size of space, in 2003 the Hubble Telescope focused southwest of the Orion constellation at a spot where there was nothing – a spot equivalent in size to a grain of sand held out at arms-length. After weeks of exposure, an image was compiled called the Hubble Deep Space Field, which revealed the spot contained over 10,000 galaxies. And that spot was just one 30 millionth of the sky.

Telescope exposures in every directions yielded similar discoveries. With light consisting of different colored wavelengths that travel at different speeds, the Hubble telescope data was fed into a computer and rendered into a 3-D film. What the viewer sees is not an artist's rendition, but the actual galaxies billions of light years away.

Sir William Blackstone wrote in *Commentaries on the Laws of England*, 1768:

> When the Supreme Being formed the universe, and created matter out of nothing, He impressed certain principles upon that matter … certain laws of motion, to which all movable bodies must conform … not left to chance … but … guided by unerring rules laid down by the great Creator.

Either this immense and complex universe happened by illogical random chance, and therefore there is no purpose to anything, or there exists an incomprehensibly powerful Creator who has a purpose for everything He created, including each person.

> Psalms 8:3–4 "When I consider thy heavens, the work of thy fingers, the moon and the stars, which thou hast ordained; What is man, that thou art mindful of him? and the son of man, that thou visitest him?"

NICOLAUS COPERNICUS

The Scientific Revolution is considered to have begun when Nicolaus Copernicus published his 1542 work *On the Revolutions of the Heavenly Spheres.*

Born in Poland, Copernicus followed in the footsteps of previous astronomers:, such as: Aristarchus of Samos (c.310–230 BC); Hipparchus (c.190 BC–c.120 BC); Ptolemy (c.90–c.168 AD); Aryabhata (476–550); Al-Kindi (c.801–c.873); Bhaskara (1114–1185); and Nasir al-Din al-Tusi (1201–1274).

Copernicus (1473–1543) discovered that the planets did not revolve around the Earth, as in astronomer Ptolemy's geocentric theory, but instead the Earth, as well as all the other planets in the solar system, revolved around the Sun at the center, heliocentric.

Having a doctorate in cannon church law, he wrote: "The Universe – wrought for us by a supremely good and orderly Creator."

Copernicus stated:

To know the mighty works of God, to comprehend His wisdom and majesty and power; to appreciate, in degree, the wonderful workings of His laws, surely all this must be a pleasing and acceptable mode of worship to the Most High, to whom ignorance cannot be more grateful than knowledge.

He added:

I am aware that a philosopher's ideas are not subject to the judgment of ordinary persons, because it is his endeavor to seek the truth in all things, to the extent permitted to human reason by God.

The Book of Isaiah 45:12, states:

Thus saith the Lord, the Holy One of Israel ... I, even my hands, have stretched out the heavens.

ℭℛ

GALILEO GALILEI

Italian astronomer Galileo Galilei (1564–1642) was the first astronomer to use a telescope, which he built himself in 1609.

His observations supported Copernicus' heliocentric theory. He confirmed the phases of Venus, discovered four of Jupiter's moons, observed Saturn's rings, and analyzed sunspots.

Galilei stated:

• Mathematics is the language in which God has written the universe.

• I give infinite thanks to God, who has been pleased to make me the first observer of marvelous things.

• The laws of nature are written by the Hand of God in the language of mathematics.

• God is known by nature in His works, and by doctrine in His revealed Word.

• The prohibition of science would be contrary to the Bible which in hundreds of places teaches us how the greatness and glory of God shine forth marvelously in all His works, and is to be read above all in the open book of the heavens.

Galileo stated:

I am inclined to think that the authority of Holy Scripture is intended to convince men of those truths which are necessary for their salvation, which, being far above man's understanding, cannot be made credible by any learning, or any other means than revelation by the Holy Spirit.

Galileo's work gave credence to Copernicus' heliocentric theory, which was further advanced by Tycho Brahe and Johannes Kepler.

"The heavens proclaim His righteousness"–Psalm 50:6;

"The heavens declare the glory of God"–Psalm 19:1.

CR

TYCHO BRAHE

Danish astronomer Tycho Brahe (1546–1601) was the last major naked-eye astronomer, who compiled very accurate astronomical and planetary observations.

Tycho Brahe stated:

> Those who study the stars have God for a teacher.

Brahe wrote in *On Recent Phenomena in the Aetherial World*, 1588:

> That the machine of Heaven is ... divinely governed under a given law.

In observing a super nova, Tycho Brahe wrote *On the New Star*, 1573:

> I noticed that a new and unusual star, surpassing all others in brilliancy ... it was quite evident to me that there had never before been any star in that place in the sky ... A miracle indeed, either the greatest of all that have occurred in the whole range of nature since the beginning of the world, or one certainly that is to be classed with those attested by the Holy Oracles.

King James I and his bride, Princess Anne, visited Tycho Brahe while in Denmark for their wedding. After Brahe's death, Kepler continued making astronomical observations.

☙

JOHANNES KEPLER

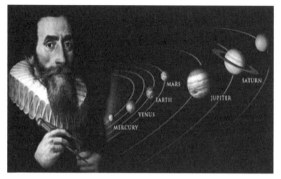

Johannes Kepler was born December 27, 1571. An attack of smallpox when he was four years old left him with crippled hands and poor eyesight.

He overcome these handicaps, and originally studied to be a priest at the University of Tübingen. He was drawn to study of science, and at age 23, became a professor of astronomy.

In 1600, Kepler traveled to Prague where he became an assistant to the Danish astronomer Tycho Brahe, who was known for his comprehensive astronomical and planetary observations.

Johannes Kepler discovered the laws governing planetary motion and pioneered the discipline of celestial mechanics, known as Kepler's Laws. These aided Isaac Newton in his formulation of the theories of gravitation, motion and calculus.

Kepler explained:

> • I believe only and alone in the service of Jesus Christ. In him is all refuge and solace.

> • Science is the process of thinking God's thoughts after Him.

Kepler wrote:

• The chief aim of all investigations of the external world should be to discover the rational order and harmony which has been imposed on it by God and which He revealed to us in the language of mathematics.

• The wisdom of the Lord is infinite as are also His glory and His power. Ye heavens, sing His praises; sun, moon, and planets, glorify Him in your ineffable language! Praise Him, celestial harmonies, and all ye who can comprehend them! And thou, my soul, praise thy Creator! It is by Him and in Him that all exist.

Johannes Kepler remarked:

Since we astronomers are priests of the highest God in regard to the book of nature, it befits us to be thoughtful, not of the glory of our minds, but rather, above all else, of the glory of God.

He stated:

It is a right, yes a duty, to search in cautious manner for the numbers, sizes, and weights, the norms for everything God has created. For He himself has let man take part in the knowledge of these things ...

For these secrets are not of the kind whose research should be forbidden; rather they are set before our eyes like a mirror so that by examining them we observe to some extent the goodness and wisdom of the Creator.

Kepler added:

Those laws are within the grasp of the human mind. God wanted us to recognize them by creating us after his own image so that we could share in his own thoughts ... and if piety allow us to say so, our understanding is in this respect of the same kind as the divine, at least as far as we are able to grasp something of it in our mortal life.

Some intellectuals in Europe attempted to use the discovery of laws in God's creation to argue that God set the laws of nature in motion, and then became distant and uninvolved – a movement called "deism."

This was not the view of Kepler, who wrote in *The Harmonies of the World,* 1619:

O, Almighty God, I am thinking Thy thoughts after Thee!

Kepler's publishing of the ephemeris tables, necessary for plotting star movement, contributed to the theory of calculus.

In comparing celestial orbits of the planets with polyphonic harmonies in music, Kepler wrote in *The Harmonies of the Worlds* (1619):

Holy Father, keep us safe in the concord of our love for one another, that we may be one just as Thou art with Thy Son, Our Lord, and with the Holy Ghost, and just as through the sweetest bonds of harmonies Thou hast made all Thy works one, and that from the bringing of Thy people into concord, the body of Thy Church may be built up in the Earth, as Thou didst erect the heavens themselves out of harmonies.

Kepler wrote:

The heavenly bodies are nothing but a continuous song for several voices (perceived by the intellect, not by the ear); a music which ... sets landmarks in the immeasurable flow of time. It is therefore, no longer surprising that man, in imitation of his Creator, has at last discovered the art of figured song, which was unknown to the ancients.

Man wanted to reproduce the continuity of cosmic time ... to obtain a sample test of the delight of the Divine Creator in His works, and to partake of his joy by making music in the imitation of God.

In the conclusion of his treatise, *The Harmonies of the Worlds* (1619), Kepler wrote:

I thank Thee, my Creator and Lord, that Thou hast given me this joy in Thy creation, this delight in the works of Thy hands; I have shown the excellency of Thy works unto man, so far as my finite mind was able to comprehend Thine infinity; if I have said aught of Thy glory, graciously forgive it.

He stated:

The cause of the six-sided shape of a snowflake is none other than that of the ordered shapes of plants and of numerical constants; and since in them nothing occurs without supreme reason – not, to be sure, such as discursive reasoning discovers, but such as existed from the first in the Creator's design and is preserved from that origin to this day in the wonderful nature of animal faculties,

I do not believe that even in a snowflake this ordered pattern exists at random.

Two centuries later, Yale professor Benjamin Silliman, who in 1818 founded the *American Journal of Science and Arts*, stated:

The relation of geology, as well as astronomy, to the Bible, when both are well understood, is that of perfect harmony ... The Word and the works of God cannot conflict, and the more they are studied the more perfect will their harmony appear.

Complex patterns in nature seemingly confirm Kepler's belief in an Intelligent Designer. One such pattern is called the "divine proportion" or Golden Ratio.

Kepler's study of this ratio is a geometric progression called a Kepler Triangle. This irrational ratio, also called phi, is expressed as the decimal number 1.618.

Expressed as an equation, it is called the Fibonacci sequence, where, beginning with zero, each subsequent number is the sum of the previous two. Greek mathematician Euclid explained it as when a line is cut in two, and "the whole line is to the greater segment, so is the greater to the lesser."

The Golden Ratio is observed in extremely complex geometric patterns called fractals, where each part has the same statistical character as the whole. It is displayed everything from atoms to galaxies, snowflakes, crystals, to the petals of a rose and seeds in sunflowers and pine cones.

It exists in nautilus seashells and seahorse tails, from fish scales, to snake skins, to bird feathers, to the dimensional shape of an egg. It is observed in fluid turbulence, from the vortex of water going down a drain, to ocean waves, to hurricanes and tornadoes, and to the twisted shape of a DNA molecule.

Another unique aspect of the universe was noted by physicist Stephen Hawkins in *A Brief History of Time* (1996, p. 126):

If the rate of expansion one second after the Big Bang had been smaller by even one part in a hundred thousand million million, it would have recollapsed before it reached its present size.

On the other hand, if it had been greater by a part in a million, the universe would have expanded too rapidly for stars and planets to form.

There are 100s of parameters which all must be present for life to exist on Earth, such as:

• If the Sun's gravitational pull was not balanced with the centrifugal force of the Earth spinning in orbit, the Earth would either be pulled into the Sun or fly off into space;

• If the Earth were 2 percent closer to the Sun it would be scorched and if it were 2 percent further away from the Sun it would be frozen.

• If the Earth did not have a molten core, there would be no magnetic field to protect the surface from deadly cosmic radiation;

• If Jupiter, the largest planet in the solar system – with a mass 2.5 times all the other planets combined – was not exerting its immense gravitational pull, comets and asteroids from space would strike the Earth;

• If the Earth took longer to rotate, increased Sun exposure would make it inhospitable;

• If the Earth did not have a tilt, there would be no seasons;

• If the Moon did not exist, the oceans would wash over the face of the Earth;

• If the Moon were not in its exact position, there would not be the precise gravitational pull necessary for the Earth's ocean tides.

Best-selling author Eric Metaxas wrote in the *The Wall Street Journal* article "Science Increasingly Makes the Case for God" (Dec. 25, 2014):

> In 1966 ... astronomer Carl Sagan announced that there were two important criteria for a planet to support life: The right kind of star, and a planet the right distance from that star.
>
> Given the roughly octillion – 1 followed by 24 zeros – planets in the universe, there should have been about septillion – 1 followed by 21 zeros – planets capable of supporting life ...
>
> But as years passed, the silence from the rest of the universe was deafening ... As of 2014, researchers have discovered precisely bubkis – 0 followed by nothing ...

Metaxas continued:

> What happened? As our knowledge of the universe increased, it became clear that there were far more factors necessary for life than Sagan supposed. His two parameters grew to 10 and then 20 and then 50, and so the number of potentially life-supporting planets decreased accordingly ...
>
> Peter Schenkel wrote in a 2006 piece for *Skeptical Inquirer* magazine: "In light of new findings ... we should quietly admit that the early estimates ... may no longer be tenable."

He stated further:

> As factors continued to be discovered, the number of possible planets hit zero ... In other words, the odds turned against any planet in the universe supporting life, including this one ... Today there are more than 200 known parameters necessary

for a planet to support life – every single one of which must be perfectly met, or the whole thing falls apart.

Without a massive planet like Jupiter nearby, whose gravity will draw away asteroids, a thousand times as many would hit Earth's surface. The odds against life in the universe are simply astonishing. Yet here we are, not only existing, but talking about existing.

What can account for it? ... At what point is it fair to admit that science suggests that we cannot be the result of random forces? ...

Eric Metaxas ended:

Theoretical physicist Paul Davies has said that "the appearance of design is overwhelming" ... Oxford professor Dr. John Lennox has said "the more we get to know about our universe, the more the hypothesis that there is a Creator ... gains in credibility as the best explanation of why we are here."

Don Brownlee, Professor of Astronomy at the University of Washington in Seattle, stated:

If you think of the universe as a whole, it's almost a totally hostile place ... The Earth is undoubtedly rare in the solar system.

Actor Leonardo DiCaprio agreed, stating in 2016:

We've been given this gift, our planet, and we've found no other place in the universe that we can inhabit.

In book five of *The Harmonies of the World* (1619), Kepler wrote:

The die is cast; the book is written, to be read either now or by posterity, I care not which. It may be well to wait a century for a reader, as God has waited six thousand years for an observer.

Sir William Blackstone wrote in *Commentaries on the Laws of England*, 1768:

Man, the noblest of all sublunary (earthly) beings, a creature endowed with both reason and free will … depends absolutely upon his Maker for everything … It is necessary that he should in all points conform to his Maker's will … These are the eternal, immutable laws of good and evil, to which the Creator Himself in all his dispensations conforms; and which He has enabled human reason to discover.

Scriptures proclaim:

• Jeremiah 32:17: "Ah Lord God! behold, Thou hast made the heaven and the earth by Thy great power and stretched out arm, and there is nothing too hard for Thee."

• Psalm 33:6: "By the word of the LORD were the heavens made; and all the host of them by the breath of His mouth."

• Job 26:7: "He spreads out the northern skies over empty space; He suspends the earth over nothing."

Johannes Kepler, wrote:

I had the intention of becoming a theologian … but now I see how God is, by my endeavors, also glorified in astronomy, for "the heavens declare the glory of God."

ॐ

HISTORY OF WRITING
& ANCIENT ISRAEL

Human knowledge was able to be accumulated and passed on to future generations through the invention of "writing," begun around 3300 BC.

Richard Overy, editor of *The Times Complete History of the World*, stated in "The 50 Key Dates of World History" (October 19, 2007):

> No date appears before the start of human civilizations about 5,500 years ago and the beginning of a written or pictorial history.

The earliest human records appear in Sumerian cuneiform on clay tablets in the Mesopotamian Valley. Astrophysicist Neil deGrasse Tyson stated in the *Cosmos* TV series (2014, natgeotv.com, episode 10, "The Immortals"):

> It was the people who once lived here, around 5,000 years ago, who first started chopping up time into smaller bite-size portions of hours and minutes. They call this place Uruk. We call it Iraq. The part of Mesopotamia – the land between the Tigris and Euphrates Rivers. The "city" was invented here. And one of humanities greatest victories was won over the ceaseless battle of time. It was here that we learned how to write.

Writing was first on pieces of clay, then on papyrus reeds from the Nile Delta, notably Egyptian hieroglyphics, appearing around 3,000 BC. The reeds, which grew 16 feet tall, had their outer rind removed, leaving the sticky inner cores, which were cut into strips, interwoven together, soaked, pressed, and then dried.

The word "paper" comes from the word "papyrus." It was the main medium to write upon for nearly 3,000 years.

China's writing with pictogram characters was invented around 2,600 BC during the reign of the legendary Yellow Emperor. Instead of using reeds, the Chinese used bamboo, which was cut into strips and written upon vertically. These strips were tied together creating bamboo annals or books.

The earliest Indus Valley markings were during the Harappan civilization, somewhere around 2,600 BC, along the Indus River Valley in Punjab and Sindh. Harappan writing has never been deciphered.

Writing was also upon palm leaves, bark, bones, and stone. It was then made on parchment made from the skins of sheep and goats, and on vellum made from calfskin.

Writing originated as an accounting method which scribes used to keep track of everything the king owned. Then writing was used to keep record of a king's decrees or a king's genealogy, as well as astronomical observations.

In ancient Egypt with an overall literacy rate of less than one percent, only kings, upper class, and scribes could read. It was their secret knowledge.

The National Archaeological Museum in Athens, Greece, in its section on Egyptian Artifacts, has a display on "Scribes," stating:

> Only a small percentage of ancient Egypt's population was literate, namely the pharaoh, members of the royal family, officials, priests and scribes. Particularly popular and lucrative, the scribe's profession was mostly hereditary. Scribes had careers in the government, priesthood, and army. They began their rigorous training in their early childhood. Most of their training took place inside a building called the "House of Life," attached to the temple. Scribes wrote on stone or clay sherds.

Reading and writing was, for the most part, the communication of the deep-state ruling elite class who wanted to control the ignorant and uneducated masses. Anthropologist Claude Levi Strauss (1908–2008) wrote:

> Ancient writing's main function was to facilitate the enslavement of other human beings.

Facilitating government's control over the illiterate masses was the fact that the thousands of cuneiform, hieroglyphic and pictogram characters were difficult to learn. In addition to that, lower classes and slaves were not allowed to learn them. Kings wanted subjects to blindly obey, not think for themselves.

James Madison wrote to W.T. Barry, August 4, 1822: "Knowledge will forever govern ignorance." George Orwell wrote in *Nineteen Eighty-Four:*

> In the long run, a hierarchical society was only possible on a basis of poverty and ignorance.

Scribes kept meticulous court records to track of a king's treasures, decrees, genealogies, astronomical observations, myths, and royal propaganda. An early form of fake news in Egypt was that scribes would omit military losses, rebellions, or anything that would portray a pharaoh negatively.

In order to carry out a king's will, some in the administrative class and military class were granted security clearances to learn the secret of reading and writing.

Writing was the equivalent of the high-tech industry. Elite ruling classes always kept common people and slaves uninformed, prohibiting them from being educated or from communicating.

Rather than educating subjects and trusting them with information, kings controlled through honor and shame, rewarding those who obeyed them and shaming those who do not. If that was not sufficient, kings and despots used pleasure pain, rewarding loyalty and 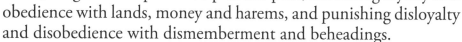 obedience with lands, money and harems, and punishing disloyalty and disobedience with dismemberment and beheadings.

The first well-recorded instance of a nation, with millions of people, ruling itself without a king was ancient Israel when it made its exodus from Egypt's Pharaoh around 1,400 BC.

When Moses came down Mount Sinai, he not only had the Law, he had it in a 22 character alphabet that was so easy to comprehend that even children learned to read.

The first letter was "aleph," second letter "beth," etc. Levites taught the people the law and taught them how to read the law. Ancient Israel is, perhaps, the first instance in history of where the general population was literate. Jewish historian Eupolemus wrote c.150 BC:

> Moses was the first wise man. He taught the alphabet to the Jews who passed it on to the Phoenicians, who passed it to the Greeks. Moses first wrote laws for the Jews.
> (cited in *Praeparatio Evangelica*, 9:26.1, by Eusebius of Caesarea, 4th century AD)

Not only could they read the Law, they were required to, as the Law was addressed to each individual citizen. E.C. Wines wrote in *The Hebrew Republic* (Philadelphia: c1853):

> A fundamental principle of the Hebrew government was ... the education of the whole body of the people ... An ignorant people cannot be a free people. Intelligence is essential to liberty. No nation is capable of self-government, which is not educated to understand and appreciate its responsibilities ...

> Upon this principle Moses proceeded in the framing of his commonwealth ... There is reason to believe that the ability to read and write was an accomplishment more generally possessed by the Hebrews than by any other people of antiquity.

Wherever there is a king, the friends of the king are "more equal" and those not friends with the king are "less equal." Those who are enemies of the king are dead – it is called "treason," or they are slaves.

For Israel's first four centuries in the Promised Land, there was no king, being ruled instead by the Law. The Law declared there was no respect of persons in judgment; rich and poor were to be treated the same; male and female made in the image of the Creator; even the stranger living among them was under the same Law that they were under.

This was the beginning of the concept of "equality" as there was no royal family to seek favors from – no superior or inferior class, no caste system.

Israel's experiment in self-government was dependent on one thing – the priests teaching the people to read the Law. People were motivated to keep the Law as they were taught:

1) there is a God who is everywhere, who knows every thought and sees every action;

2) God wants them to be fair;

3) God will hold each person accountable in the future.

When the priests neglected teaching the Law, everyone did what was right in their own eyes and the country fell into moral chaos.

The Hebrew Republic ended when the people sinned by asking for a king. Out of their rebellious moral chaos, Israel got a totalitarian ruler, King Saul, who soon killed a large number of the priests, with the exception of Abiathar escaping to David.

The pattern was clear – for a country to maintain order without fear of a king, there needed to be a citizenry educated in moral restraints, who obeyed out of fear of God.

∝℞

HISTORY OF PRINTING

In 221 BC, China's Warring States Period ended with the victory of Qin Shi Huangdi, considered the first emperor of China.

When he was criticized for doing things differently than they had been done in the past, Qin Shi Huangdi ordered all the hand-written records of the past to be burned and the scholars buried.

The Basic Annals of the First Emperor of Qin reported that Qin's Chancellor, Li Si, told the Emperor in 213 BC:

> I, your servant, propose that all historians' records other than those of Qin's be burned ... If anyone under heaven has copies of the Classics of History (Shu Jing) ... they shall deliver them to the governor ... for burning. Anyone who dares to discuss the Classics of History shall be publicly executed.

> Anyone who uses history to criticize the present shall have his family executed ... Anyone who has failed to burn the books after thirty days of this announcement shall be subjected to tattooing and be sent to build the Great Wall.

Similarly, Islamic Caliphs conquered territories, then burned libraries and forbade followers from reading the Bible. Thomas Aquinas wrote of Mohammed in *Summa contra Gentiles*, 1258:

> It was a shrewd decision on his part to forbid his followers to read the Old and
> New Testaments, lest these books convict him of falsity.

The invention of printing led to knowledge and information becoming accessible by more people.

After China's Qin Dynasty was overthrown, and the Han Dynasty began to rule in 202 BC, Chinese scribes developed the process of making paper from tree pulp and rags.

In 175 AD, Han Dynasty scribes placed paper over stone engravings of texts of Confucius and made rubbings with charcoal. This developed into laying paper over raised stone letters covered with ink, a technique which spread to other countries like Japan, where a Nara Empress printed a Buddhist charm in 768 AD.

Using a method with carved wooden or baked clay blocks, China, during the Tang Dynasty, created what could be considered the first "printed" book in 868 AD.

In China, Bi Sheng invented movable type printing with porcelain characters during the Song Dynasty, 1041, leading to China being the first country to have printed "paper currency."

Printing of currency, using copper plates, occurred on a mass scale during Kublai Khan's Yuan Dynasty, 1215–1294, even being mentioned by Marco Polo. China's over-printing of currency led to it being devalued, resulting in inflation and economic collapse.

Ultimately, the currency depreciated by 1,000 percent causing the country to become politically unstable. This contributed to ending the Mongolian Yuan Dynasty in 1368.

The shear number of Chinese characters, over 50,000, discouraged China from making further printing innovations.

In 1234, Korea's Goryeo Dynasty invented the first "metal" movable type printing press. In 1443, Korean Emperor Sejong the Great introduced a 24-letter han'gul alphabet which made printing practical.

Whereas China used pictogram characters, and Egypt used hieroglyphs, Western Civilization had been using a phonetic characters dating back to a Semitic alphabet around 1500 BC.

It was not until 1400 AD that Europeans first began using carved wooden blocks applied with ink to print religious messages.

℘

JOHANNES GUTENBERG & THE PRINTING PRESS

In Germany, Johannes Gutenberg invented a printing press – the Western world's first "metal moveable type" printing press.

On August 24, 1455, Gutenberg printed his masterpiece, the Gutenberg Bible, regarded as the first book of significance ever printed. No longer copied tediously by the hands of scribes, Bibles were soon mass produced.

Gutenberg, whose name means "beautiful mountain," wrote about his 42-line Gutenberg Bible, also called the Mazarin Bible, 1455:

> God suffers in the multitude of souls whom His word cannot reach. Religious truth is imprisoned in a small number of manuscript books which confine instead of spread the public treasure.

> Let us break the seal which seals up holy things and give wings to Truth in order that she may win every soul that comes into the world by her word no longer written at great expense by hands easily palsied, but multiplied like the wind by an untiring machine ...

Gutenberg continued:

> Yes, it is a press, certainly, but a press from which shall flow in inexhaustible streams the most abundant and most marvelous liquor that has ever flowed to relieve the thirst of men. Through it, God will spread His word; a spring of pure truth shall flow from it; like a new star it shall scatter the darkness of ignorance, and cause a light hithertofore unknown to shine among men.

In March of 1455, future Pope Pius II commented on Gutenberg's Bible in a letter to Cardinal Carvajal:

> All that has been written to me about that marvelous man seen at Frankfurt is true. I have not seen complete Bibles but only a number of quires of various books of the Bible. The script was very neat and legible, not at all difficult to follow – your grace would be able to read it without effort, and indeed without glasses.

Unfortunately for Gutenberg, he had borrowed 8,000 guilders from Johann Fust, who sued him at the archbishop's court in 1456 and took the print shop, leaving Gutenberg bankrupt. Gutenberg re-started a smaller print shop and participated in printing Bibles in the town of Bamberg.

The word "Bible" comes from the Greek word "biblia" meaning books, as it is a collection of many Old Testament and New Testament books, bound together in one volume.

From 382 AD to the Renaissance and Reformation, there have been typically 73 books in the Bible. The Eastern Orthodox Bible has 78, the Geneva Bible has 80, and the Ethiopian

Bible has 81. In 1625, the King James Bible was revised to the number to 66 books.

Since Gutenberg's invention of the printing press in mid-1400's, the HOLY BIBLE has been THE MOST PRINTED BOOK IN ALL OF WORLD HISTORY, estimated at over 6 billion copies.

On August 12, 1993, Pope John Paul II gave a rare copy of the Gutenberg Bible to President Bill Clinton at Denver's Regis University in Colorado.

Woodrow Wilson stated at the 300th Anniversary of the Translation of the King James Bible in the English Language, May 7, 1911:

> I wonder how many persons in this great audience realize the significance for English-speaking peoples of the translation of the Bible into the English tongue.
>
> Up to the time of the translation of the Bible into English, it was a book for long ages withheld from the perusal of the peoples of other languages ...
>
> Not a little of the history of liberty lies in the circumstance that the moving sentences of this Book were made familiar to the ears and the understanding of those peoples who have led mankind in exhibiting the forms of government and the impulses of reform which have made for freedom and for self-government among mankind ...

Wilson continued:

> For this is a book which reveals men unto themselves, not as creatures ... under human authority ... It reveals every man to himself as a distinct moral agent,

responsible not to men, not even to those men whom he has put over him in authority, but responsible through his own conscience to his Lord and Maker. Whenever a man sees this vision he stands up a free man.

Franklin D. Roosevelt stated October 6, 1935:

The four hundredth anniversary of the printing of the first English Bible is an event of great significance ... The ... influence of this greatest of books ... so greatly affected the progress of Christian civilization ...

This Book continues to hold its unchallenged place as the most loved, the most quoted and the most universally read and pondered of all the volumes ... It continues to hold its supreme place as the Book of books ...

FDR concluded:

We cannot read the history of our rise and development as a Nation, without reckoning with the place the Bible has occupied in shaping the advances of the Republic ... Its teaching ... is ploughed into the very heart of the race. Where we have been truest and most consistent in obeying its precepts we have attained the greatest measure of contentment and prosperity.

Gutenberg's invention was considered the most important event of the modern period as it began a printing revolution which spread knowledge, information and ideas at an unprecedented speed. It fueled Europe's Renaissance, Reformation, and the Scientific Revolution. Napoleon introduced the printing press to Egypt when he invaded in 1798.

No longer was knowledge and information solely under the control of the ruling class establishment.

Later generations experienced innovations whereby individuals could communicate information with large numbers of people through theater, music, talk radio, television, telephone, and the internet. Unfortunately, with each new method of sharing information came new attempts by powerful deep state elites to regulate and control it.

Victor Hugo wrote in *The Hunchback of Notre Dame*, 1831, book 5:

> The 15th century everything changes. Human thought discovers a mode of perpetuating itself ... Gutenberg's letters of lead ... supersede Orpheus's letters of stone ...

> The invention of printing is the greatest event in history. It is the mother of revolution ... Whether it be Providence or Fate, Gutenberg is the precursor of Luther.

In *A Tramp Abroad*, 1880, Mark Twain wrote:

> We made a short halt at Frankfort-on-the-Main ... I would have liked to visit the birthplace of Gutenberg, but ... no memorandum of the house has been kept.

JULIAN CALENDAR & ANNO DOMINI

Ancient peoples throughout the Mediterranean, North Africa, the Middle East and Europe, had used calendars based on the moon from the beginning of recorded history. These lunar calendars had the seasons cycle incrementally through the months, gradually shifting through the years, decades and centuries as an enormous multi-generational clock.

As the Roman Empire expanded and conquered nations, these lunar calendars were difficult to reconcile with each other.

In 45 BC, Julius Caesar was the Roman Emperor. He acted, in a sense, as the first globalist. He wanted a calendar to organize and unify the Roman world, so he replaced the many lunar calendars with a new solar calendar based on the sun. This was called the "Julian Calendar."

The Julian Calendar had 365 days and an extra "leap" day every 4th year, at the end of February. Rome's old fifth month, Quintilis, was renamed after Julius Caesar, being called "July." As it only had 30 days, a day was taken from the old end of the year, February, and added to the month of July, giving it 31 days.

The next emperor, Augustus Caesar, renamed the old sixth month, Sextilis, after himself, calling it "August." He also took a day from the old end of the year, February, and added it to August, giving that month 31 days and leaving February with only 28 days.

Julius Caesar also made January the first month of the year. Previously, March had been the first month. Remnants of March being the first month is still seen in the old Latin names of the months: September, October, November, December.

- "Sept" is Latin for seven;
- "Oct" is Latin for eight (i.e. octagon = eight sided);
- "Nov" is Latin for nine; and
- "Dec" is Latin for ten (i.e. decimal = divisible by ten).

Julius Caesar's successor was Augustus Caesar, who wanted to further organize the empire by setting up a world-wide government tracking system.

Luke 2:1–3 recorded:

> And it came to pass in those days that a decree went out from Caesar Augustus that all the world should be registered. This census first took place while Quirinius was governing Syria.

For the first three centuries of Christianity, Christians were persecuted throughout the Roman Empire in ten major persecutions. Finally, Emperor Constantine ended the persecutions in 313 AD, and effectively made Christianity the recognized religion of the Empire.

Just as Julius Caesar unified the Roman Empire with the Julian Calendar, Constantine decided to unify the Christian Roman Empire with a common date for celebrating Easter, the Resurrection of Christ, which was the most important event in the Christian calendar.

Providentially, Jesus had been crucified as the "Passover Lamb" on the exact date the Jews were celebrating the Feast of Passover. Passover commemorated the night in Egypt when Angel of Death passed over the homes of the Israelites who put the blood of the lamb over their doorposts.

The Apostle Paul wrote in I Corinthians 5:7

> For even Christ our Passover is sacrificed for us.

The next day the Jews celebrated the Feast of Unleavened Bread. Leaven, or yeast, was symbolic of sin, and on this day Jews removed all the leaven from their homes.

I Corinthians 5:6–8:

> Know ye not that a little leaven leaveneth the whole lump? Purge out therefore the old leaven ... let us keep the feast, not with the old leaven, neither with the leaven of malice and wickedness; but with the unleaven bread of sincerity and truth.

Jesus, "who taketh away the sins of the world" and was in the tomb on the exact date of the Jewish Feast of Unleavened Bread.

Next, the Jews celebrated the Feast of First Fruits – the beginning of the barley harvest, when the first shoots of the newly planted crops appeared above ground. Jesus rose from the dead on the exact date of Jews celebrated the Feast of First Fruits

I Corinthians 15:20–23:

But now is Christ risen from the dead and become the first fruits of them that slept ... But every man in his own order: Christ the first fruits; afterward they that are Christ's at his coming.

George Washington's tomb is engraved with the Scripture, John 11:25, where Jesus told Martha:

I am the Resurrection and the Life; sayeth the Lord. He that believeth in Me, though he were dead yet shall he live. And whosoever liveth and believeth in Me shall never die.

President Ronald Reagan stated in his Easter Address, April 2, 1983:

This week Jewish families and friends have been celebrating Passover ... and Christians have been commemorating the last momentous days leading to the crucifixion of Jesus 1,950 years ago.

Tomorrow, as morning spreads around the planet, we'll celebrate the triumph of life over death, the Resurrection of Jesus ... Both observances tell of sacrifice and pain but also of hope and triumph ... Men and women around the world ... bear a message of world hope ... like the rites of Passover and Easter that we celebrate this weekend.

President Donald Trump stated March 31, 2018:

During the sacred holiday of Passover, Jewish families around the world give thanks to God for liberating the Jewish people from bondage in Egypt and for delivering them to the Promised Land of Israel.

For Christians, we remember the suffering and death of God's only Son and his glorious resurrection on the third day. On Easter Sunday, we proclaim with joy ... Christ is Risen!

Both of these sacred celebrations remind us that God's love redeems the world. Almost 3,000 years ago, the prophet Isaiah wrote, "Darkness covers the earth, but the Lord rises upon you and his Glory appears over you. For the Lord will be your everlasting light" ...

We praise our Heavenly Father for the blessings of freedom and the gift of eternal life. Happy Passover. Happy Easter ... and God bless America.

In 325 AD, Emperor Constantine called all the church leaders to assemble at the Council of Nicaea, where, among other things, he proposed that the Resurrection, or Easter, be celebrated throughout the Roman Empire on a Sunday.

This was the beginning of the split between what had been a predominately Jewish Christian Church – as Jesus and his disciples were Jewish – and the emerging Gentile Christian Church.

Prior to this, each year, Christians would ask Jewish rabbis when the Passover Feast would be celebrated according to the Hebrew lunar calendar, on the evening of 14th day of the month Nissan, which could fall on any day of the week.

Constantine's insistence of Easter being on Sunday necessitated a new formula to determine the date of Easter, namely, the first Sunday after the First Paschal Full Moon falling on or after the Spring Equinox.

"Equinox" is a solar calendar term: "equi" = "equal" and "nox" = "night." Thus "equinox" is when the daytime and nighttime are of equal duration. It occurs in the Spring around March 20 and in the Autumn around September 22.

In the year 325 AD, Easter was on March 21. During the Middle Ages, France celebrated its New Year's Day on Easter. Tables were compiled to forecast the future dates of Easter.

Another calendar item of interest was the numbering of years. Years were historically recorded in relation to the reign of kings, such as II Kings 18:10 "In the sixth year of King Hezekiah of Judah, that is the ninth year of Hoshea king of Israel"; or Luke 3:1 "Now in the fifteenth year of the reign of Tiberius Caesar."

In 526 AD, in the reign of Emperor Justinian, a scholarly monk named Dionysius Exigus thought it inappropriate that the Christian Roman Empire was still recording dates in relation to the reign of anti-Christian Emperor Diolcetian – "Anno Diocletiani," as he had perpetrated the most severe persecution of Christians, 303–311 AD.

The monk Dionysius Exigus began making notations in his writings, marking down dates in relation to the birth of Jesus Christ – "Anno Domini," which in Latin means "in the year of the Lord's reign."

Gradually, this method of recording dates was used in Church records, and eventually became the most accepted dating system in the world. All dates in world history are either BC "Before Christ" or AD "Anno Domini" – meaning in the Year of the Lord's Reign.

Clarence E. Manion, dean of the Notre Dame Law School, stated:

B.C. (before Christ) and A.D. (Anno Domini, the year of our Lord) mark each one of the only reliable milestones along the path of world history ... The end of the first time-chain, and the beginning of the second, came together on the night that Christ was born in Bethlehem ...

The first Christmas Day thus stands as the Great Divide for the timing and recording of all people, things and events that have lived or taken place upon this earth ... It is ... the one place on the long, long trail of time where the magnetic needle of history stands vertical and points up.

In the late 19th century, secularists in academia popularized the use of BCE – "Before Common Era" and CE "Common Era."

The futile nature of this is displayed by the question: When did the recording of time change from Before Common Era to Common Era? The answer is: the birth of Christ. In the attempt to erase Christ, He is nevertheless acknowledged.

In 567 AD, the Council of Tours returned the first month of the year back to March, as the date of January 1st was associated with pagan Rome.

The Council of Tours also settled another controversy which existed between Eastern and Western Europe. The East celebrated Epiphany, January 6, as the holiest day of the season, while the West celebrated Christmas, December 25, as the holiest day.

"Epiphany" is a Greek word meaning "appearance" or "manifestation." Epiphany is also

Three Kings Day, commemorating the visit of the Wise Men to Jesus in the manger – his "manifestation" to the Gentiles, as foretold in Isaiah 49:6:

> I will also give thee for a light to the Gentiles, that thou mayest be my salvation unto the end of the earth.

In addition, Epiphany commemorates Jesus' baptism by John the Baptist in the Jordan River, as recorded in John 1:29–34:

> The next day John seeth Jesus coming unto him, and saith, Behold the Lamb of God, which taketh away the sin of the world ... He should be made manifest to Israel ... Upon whom thou shalt see the Spirit descending, and remaining on him, the same is he which baptizeth with the Holy Ghost. And I saw, and bare record that this is the Son of God.

The East and the West could not agree on which day was holier, Christmas or Epiphany, so at the Council of Tours in 567 AD, the decision was made to make all 12 days from December 25 to January 6 "The Twelve Days of Christmas." They were "holy days," which came to be pronounced "holidays."

Differences in the dates of celebrating various holy days was a source of conflict throughout Church history. For example, the date of Easter in Celtic Christian tradition was different from that of Roman Christian tradition.

The Irish strongly held to their date for Easter in the Celtic calendar, as it was the night before Easter c.433 AD, that Saint Patrick confronted the Druid chieftain King Loigaire

(Leary), resulting in him converting along with a large number of Irish.

It was not until 664 AD, at the Synod of Whitby Abbey, that King Oswy of Northumbria agreed to have the Celtic Church calendar be subordinate to the Roman Church calendar.

An interesting Leap Day event using the Julian Calendar occurred during Christopher Columbus' last voyage. Driven by storms around the Caribbean Sea, two of Columbus' ships were abandoned and the remaining two were worm-eaten and sinking. They shipwrecked on Jamaica and Indians brought his crew food for a while, but then threatened to become hostile.

Columbus, using his skill as a navigator, predicted that a lunar eclipse would take place on February 29, 1504. He called the Indian chiefs to his marooned ship and told them if they did not continue on good terms, he would pray that God would blot out the moon. When the eclipse began, the Indian chiefs shrieked and quickly made peace with Columbus.

Columbus later wrote: "My hope in the One who created us all sustains me: He is an ever-present help in trouble."

ℭℜ

GREGORIAN CALENDAR

In 1517, Luther began the Reformation resulting in German kingdoms breaking from being subordinate to the Roman Catholic Church. In 1534, England's Henry VIII broke the Anglican Church away from Rome.

As the centuries elapsed, the discrepancy between the tables listing the date of Easter on the Julian Calendar and the actual Spring equinox grew further apart.

In 1582, Pope Gregory XIII became aware that the Julian Calendar had been off by about 11 minutes per year, resulting in the compiled tables showing the date of Easter as being ten days ahead of the Spring Equinox, and even further from its origins in the Jewish Passover.

Pope Gregory XIII decided to revise the calendar by eliminating ten days. He set a leap year every 4th year with a minor adjustment: there would be NO leap day in years divisible by 100 unless it was also divisible by 400.

So there IS a leap day in the years 1600, 2000, 2400, but there is NO leap day in the years 1700, 1800, 1900, 2100, 2200, and 2300. This sounds complicated, but it is so accurate that Pope Gregory's "Gregorian Calendar" is the most internationally used calendar today.

The Gregorian Calendar also returned the beginning of the new year BACK to Julius Caesar's January 1st date. Catholic countries quickly adopted the Gregorian Calendar, but Protestant countries postponed adopting it for nearly two centuries. This gave rise to some interesting record keeping.

For example: ships would leave Protestant England on one date according to the Julian Calendar, called "Old Style" and arrive in Catholic Europe at an earlier date, as much of Europe was using the Gregorian Calendar, called "New Style."

Another example is that England's William Shakespeare and Spain's Miguel de Cervantes, author of *Man of La Mancha,* both died on the same date, April 23, 1616, but when the differences between England's Julian Calendar and Spain's Gregorian Calendar are factored in, Cervantes actually died ten days before Shakespeare.

In 1752, England and its colonies finally adopted the Gregorian Calendar, but by that time there was an 11 day discrepancy between the "Old Style" (OS) and the "New Style" (NS). America finally adjusted its calendar, so that the day after September 2, 1752 (Old Style), became September 14, 1752 (New Style). There were reportedly accounts of confusion and rioting.

As countries of Western Europe, particularly Portugal, Spain, France, the Netherlands and England, traded and established colonies around the world, they took the Gregorian Calendar with them, resulting in its international usage.

℞

SCIENTIFIC REVOLUTION & SIR FRANCIS BACON

The Renaissance of the 15th century led the Reformation of the 16th century, followed by Scientific Revolution, a period of increased understanding in the fields of astronomy, mathematics, physics, science, biology, anatomy, and chemistry, which in turn influenced philosophy. One of the individuals credited with pioneering the "scientific method" was Sir Francis Bacon (1561–1626).

Bacon was Attorney General and Lord Chancellor of Britain, being knighted in 1603 by King James I, during whose reign Jamestown, Virginia, was settled – England's first permanent settlement in the New World.

Bacon's writings were instrumental in the founding of the Royal Society of London in 1660 under King Charles II, which brought together the greatest scientific minds in England. He is quoted in the Library of Congress' Jefferson Building, on the dome above the North lobby of the Great Hall's stairway:

"KNOWLEDGE IS POWER – Sir Francis Bacon, De Hoeresibus."

Bacon advanced "inductive reasoning," where evidence is empirically and methodically observed with our senses, pointing to a probable conclusion. This is contrasted with Aristotle's "deductive reasoning," where one starts with a generalization or major hypothesis, adds minor, specifying premises, then reasonably and logically predicts what the evidence should be.

Another Bacon quote is displayed in the Library of Congress' Jefferson Building is in the West Corridor, on the South tablet:

> The first creature of God was the light of sense; the last was the light of reason.
> – Bacon, *Essays, Of Truth*.

The longer quote is:

> The first creation of God, in the works of the days, was the light of sense; the last was the light of reason, and his Sabbath work, ever since, is the illumination of the spirit.

Bacon wrote:

> There are two books laid before us to study, to prevent our falling into error; first, the volume of Scriptures, which reveal the will of God; then the volume of the Creatures, which express His power.

Bacon wrote in *Novum Organum Scientiarum*, 1620:

> Man by the Fall fell at the same time from the state of innocence and from his dominion over creation. Both of these losses, however, can even in this life be in some part repaired; the former by religion and faith, the latter by arts and sciences.

For creation was not by the curse made altogether and forever a rebel, but in virtue of that covenant "In the sweat of thy face thou shalt eat bread" it is now by various labors at length, and in some measure subdued to the supplying of man with bread; that is to the uses of human life.

Bacon wrote in *Sacred Meditations*, 1597:

God saw the works of His hands and they were exceeedingly good; when man turned to consider the works of his hands, behold all was vanity and vexation of spirit. Whereof if you will do God's works your sweat will be like aromatic balm and your rest like the Sabbath of God; for you will work in the sweat of a good conscience and rest in the leisure of sweet contemplation.

Bacon wrote in *History of the Winds*, 1623:

Without doubt we are paying for the sin of our first parents and imitating it. They wanted to be like gods; we their posterity, still more so. We create worlds. We prescribe laws to nature and lord it over her.

We want to have all things as suits our fatuity (foolishness), not as fits the Divine Wisdom, not as they are found in nature. We impose the seal of our image on the creatures and works of God, we do not diligently seek to discover the seal of God on things.

Therefore not undeservedly have we again fallen from our dominion over the creation; and though after the Fall of man some dominion over rebellious nature still remained ... we have for the most part forfeited by our pride, because we wanted to be like gods and follow the dictates of our own reason ...

He continued:

Wherefore, if there be any humility towards the Creator, if there be any reverence and praise of his works; if there be any charity towards men, and zeal to lessen human wants and sufferings; if there be any love of truth in natural things, any hatred of darkness, any desire to purify the understanding;

men are to be entreated again and again that they should dismiss ... those inconstant and preposterous philosophies ... that they should humbly and with a certain reverence draw near to the book of Creation ... that on it they should meditate, and that then washed and clean they should in chastity and integrity turn them from opinion.

This is that speech and language which has gone out to all the ends of the Earth, and has not suffered the confusion of Babel; this must men learn, and resuming their youth, they must become as little children and deign to take its alphabet into their hands.

Sir Francis Bacon wrote in *Essays: Of Goodness* (NY: Tryon Edwards, D.D., *A Dictionary of Thoughts*, Cassell Publishing Co., 1891, p. 71):

There never was found, in any age of the world, either philosophy, or sect, or religion, or law, or discipline, which did so highly exalt the good of the community, and increase private and particular good as the holy Christian faith ...

Hence, it clearly appears that it was one and the same God that gave the Christian law to men, who gave the laws of nature to the creatures.

Profound statements of Bacon include (NY: Tryon Edwards, D.D., *A Dictionary of Thoughts*, Cassell Publishing Co., 1891):

• I had rather believe all the fables in the Talmud and the Koran, than that this universal frame is without a mind.

• They that deny a God, destroy man's nobility; for clearly man is of kin to the beasts by his body, and if he be not of kin to God by his spirit, he is a base and ignoble creature.

• Knowledge is not ... for a proud mind to raise itself upon ... but a rich storehouse for the glory of the Creator, and the relief of man's estate.

Bacon wrote regarding charity in *Instauratio Magna*, 1620–1623:

I would address one general admonition to all; that they consider what are the true ends of knowledge, and that they seek it not either for pleasure of the mind, or for contention, or for superiority to others, or for profit, or fame, or power, or any of these inferior things; but for the benefit and use of life; and that they perfect and govern it in charity.

For it was from the lust of power that the angels fell, from lust of knowledge that man fell; but of charity there can be no excess, neither did angel or man ever come in danger by it.

Regarding virtue, Bacon stated (NY: Tryon Edwards, D.D., *A Dictionary of Thoughts*, Cassell Publishing Co., 1891):

- Certainly, virtue is like precious odors, most fragrant when they are incensed or crushed; for prosperity doth best discover vice, but adversity doth best discover virtue.

- A man's nature runs either to herbs or weeds; therefore let him seasonably water the one and destroy the other.

- Nuptial love maketh mankind; friendly love perfecteth it; but wanton love corrupteth and embaseth it.

- We cannot too often think there is a never-sleeping eye, which reads the heart, and registers our thoughts.

- He that studieth revenge keepeth his own wounds green, which otherwise would heal and do well.

- In revenge, a man is but even with his enemies; but it is a princely thing to pardon, for Solomon saith, "It is the glory of a man to pass over a transgression."

Regarding God and government, Bacon stated (*A Dictionary of Thoughts*, 1891):

- All precepts concerning kings are comprehended in these: remember thou are a man; remember thou art God's vice-regent.

- God hangs the greatest weights upon the smallest wires.

- There never was found, in any age of the world, either religion or law that did so highly exalt the public good as the Bible.

• When any of the four pillars of government, religion, justice, counsel, and treasure, are mainly shaken or weakened, men had need to pray for fair weather.

• If I might control the literature of the household, I would guarantee the well-being of the church and state.

Bacon wrote:

Philosophy, when superficially studied, excites doubt; when thoroughly explored, dispels it.

Regarding goodness, Bacon wrote (*The Essays of Francis Bacon*, "XIII. Of Goodness and Goodness of Nature"):

Goodness ... of all virtues ... is the greatest; being the character of the Deity: and without it man is a busy, mischievous, wretched thing; no better than a kind of vermin. Goodness answers to the theological virtue Charity ...

Goodness is imprinted deeply in the nature of man; insomuch that if it issue not towards men, it will take unto other living creatures; as it is seen in the Turks, a cruel people, who nevertheless are kind to beasts, and give alms to dogs and birds ...

Indeed there was never law, or sect, or opinion, did so much magnify goodness, as the Christian religion doth ... If a man be gracious and courteous to strangers, it shews he is a citizen of the world, and that his heart is no island cut off from other lands, but a continent that joins to them.

If he be compassionate towards the afflictions of others, it shews that his heart is like the noble tree that is wounded itself when it gives the balm. If he easily pardons and remits offenses, it shews that his mind is planted above injuries; so that he cannot be shot.

If he be thankful for small benefits, it shows that he weighs men's minds, and not their trash. But above all, if he have St. Paul's perfection, that he would wish to be an anathema from Christ for the salvation of his brethren, it shews much of a divine nature, and a kind of conformity with Christ himself.

The Scientific Revolution was advanced by the works of many notable individuals:

• Nicolas Copernicus (1473–1543) proposed the heliocentric theory of the solar system;

• Andreas Vesalius (1514–1564), founder of the modern understanding of human anatomy;

• Francois Viete (1540–1603), invented analytical trigonometry;

• William Gilbert (1544–1603,), a father of electricity and magnetism;

• Giordano Bruno (1548–1600) proposed that stars were distant suns, the universe was infinitely large, and that the Earth was not the center of it.

• John Napier (1550–1617), invented logarithms;

• Galileo Galilei (1564–1642) father of modern physics and modern observational astronomy, made the first practical use of the telescope.

- William Harvey (1578–1657), described in detail arteries, circulation and the heart;
- Zacharias Janssen (1585–1638), inventor of the optical telescope and the first truly compound microscope.
- Rene Descartes (1596–1650), father of analytical geometry and modern western philosophy;
- Otto von Guericke (1602–1686), invented the air pump;
- Giovanni Alfonso Borelli (1608–1679), father of modern biomechanics;
- Evangelista Torricelli (1608–1647), invented the mercury barometer;
- Robert Boyle (1627–1691), a father of modern chemistry;
- Anton van Leeuwenhoek (1632–1723), father of microbiology;
- Isaac Newton (1642–1727).

In his treatise *Of Atheism*, 1625, Sir Francis Bacon declared:

A little philosophy inclineth men's mind to atheism, but depth in philosophy bringeth men's minds to religion. For while the mind of man looketh upon second causes scattered, it may sometimes rest in them, and go no further. – But when it beholdeth the chain of them, confederate and linked together, it must needs fly to Providence and Deity,

⚮

ROBERT BOYLE

The "Father of Chemistry" wanted to evangelize America ... and warned of the end of the world Robert Boyle was born January 25, 1627. He studied Sir Francis Bacon, René Descartes, and other of his contemporaries of the Scientific Revolution, including:
- scientists Isaac Newton and Galileo,
- philosophers John Locke and Thomas Hobbes, and
- poet John Milton.

Robert Boyle made contributions in physics and chemistry, especially with his pneumatic experiments using the vacuum pump, putting forward the idea that gases were made of tiny particles.

He discovered the basic law of gas dynamics, known as "Boyle's Law," that if the volume of a gas is decreased, the pressure increases proportionally ($PV=c$).

An understanding of Boyle's Law is vital for scuba divers, who must never hold their breath while ascending, for as the external pressure decreases, air volume in their lungs increases, potentially causing lungs to burst like a balloon.

In 1661, Robert Boyle defined the modern idea of an "element" as "a substance that cannot be broken down into a simpler substance by a chemical reaction."

This understanding was necessary for the periodic table of elements to be compiled. Boyle's definition of "element" was used for three centuries until subatomic particles were discovered. He introduced the litmus test to distinguish acids from bases, and was the first to use the term "chemical analysis."

In 1660, Robert Boyle and eleven others formed the Royal Society in London to advance scientific experiments.

While in Geneva, Switzerland, during a frightening thunderstorm, Boyle had a deepening conversion experience. He devoted much effort to defending and propagating the Christian religion, writing the "Boyle Lectures" and numerous books, including:

- *Of the high Veneration Man's Intellect owes to God* (1684);
- *Discourse Of Things Above Reason* (1681);
- *Some Considerations touching the Style of the Holy Scriptures* (1661); and
- *The Christian Virtuoso* (1690), which John Locke reviewed in 1681, and which was a basis for Cotton Mather's work, *The Christian Philosopher* (1721).

Robert Boyle provided in his Last Will and Testament, dated July 28, 1691:

> Fifty pounds ... for an annual salary so some learned Divine or Preaching Minister ... to preach eight sermons in the year, for proving the Christian Religion against notorious Infidels, viz., Atheists, Theists, Pagans, Jews, and Mahometans, not descending lower to any controversies that are among Christians themselves ... and encouraging ... any undertaking for Propagating the Christian Religion in foreign parts.

Robert Boyle was a director of the East India Company, and spent large sums supporting missionary societies in the spread of Christianity in Asia. He believed all races, no matter how diverse, came from Adam and Eve.

He funded translations of the Bible to make it available in people's vernacular language, in contrast to the prevailing Latin-only policy. He funded an Irish edition of the Bible (1680–1685) for commoners, which was thought ill of by English upper class.

Robert Boyle was concerned about propagating the Gospel to natives in New England and the rest of America, as he wrote in a letter to Mr. Clodius. He wanted to translate and print the Bible in American Indian languages. A historical marker, "W 229 Indian School at the College of William & Mary" stated:

> Using funds from the estate of British scientist Robert Boyle, the College of William & Mary established a school to educate young Indian men ... which provided education in reading and writing English, arithmetic and religion.

Boyle wrote:

> Our Saviour would love at no less rate than death; and from the super-eminent height of glory, stooped and debased Himself to the sufferance of the extremest of indignities, and sunk himself to the bottom of abjectness, to exalt our condition to the contrary extreme.

Boyle wrote in *Some Considerations Touching the Style of the Holy Scriptures* (1661):

> The Books of Scripture ... expound each other; as in the mariner's compass, the

needle's extremity, though it seems to point purposely to the north, doth yet at the same time discover both east and west, as distant as they are from it and each other, so do some texts of Scripture guide us to the intelligence of others.

Boyle wrote:

> There are divers truths in the Christian religion, that reason left to itself would never have been able to find out ...

> Such as ... free will ... that the world was made in six days, that Christ should be born of a virgin, and that in his person there should be united two such infinitely distant natures as the divine and human; and that the bodies of good men shall be raised from death and so advantageously changed, that the glorified persons shall be like or equal to, the angels.

Boyle wrote of the last days and the "sinful world's ruin":

> In Noah's time a deluge of impiety called for a deluge of waters ... and so when (in the last days) the earth shall be replenished with those scoffers mentioned by St Peter, who will walk after their own lusts, and deride the expectation of God's foretold coming to judge and punish the ungodly, their impiety shall be as well punished as silenced by the unexpected flames ... that shall either destroy or transfigure the world.

> For as by the law of Moses the leprous garment which would not be recovered by being washed in water, was to be burnt in the fire, so the world, which the Deluge could not cleanse, a general conflagration must destroy.

Robert Boyle wrote of the destruction of the world by fire at the end of this age:

The present course of nature shall not last always, but that one day this world ... shall either be abolished by annihilation, or which seems far more probable, be innovated, and as it were transfigured, and that, by the intervention of that fire, which shall dissolve and destroy the present frame of nature: so that either way, the present state of things, (as well natural as political) shall have an end.

☙

BLAISE PASCAL

A contemporary of Robert Boyle was the French physicist, mathematician and philosopher, Blaise Pascal, born June 19, 1623. He helped develop the barometer, and pioneered hydrodynamics and fluid mechanics.

He discovered "Pascal's Principle" which is the basis of hydraulics. He is considered a father of the science of hydrostatics and hydraulic engineering.

Pascal made invaluable contributions in the

areas of probability and differential calculus, with the invention of Pascal's triangle for calculating the coefficients of a binomial expansion.

His influential religious works, emphasizing "the reasons of the heart" over dry logic and intellect, were titled *Lettres Provinciales*, 1656–57, and *Pensees Sur La Religion*, published posthumously in 1670.

In *Pensees*, 1670, Pascal wrote: "Men blaspheme what they don't know." He was known for "Pascal's Wager," which stated:

> How can anyone lose who chooses to become a Christian? If, when he dies, there turns out to be no God and his faith was in vain, he has lost nothing – in fact, he has been happier in life than his non-believing friends. If, however, there is a God and a heaven and hell, then he has gained heaven and his skeptical friends will have lost everything in hell!

In the work, *Thoughts, Letters and Opuscules*, Blaise Pascal is recorded as stating:

> We know God only through Jesus Christ. Without this Mediator, is taken away all communication with God; through Jesus Christ we know God.
>
> All those who have pretended to know God, and prove Him without Jesus Christ, have only had impotent proofs. But, to prove Jesus Christ we have the prophecies which are good and valid proofs.
>
> And those prophecies, being fulfilled, and truly proved by the event, indicate the certainty of these truths, and therefore the truth of the divinity of Jesus Christ. In

Him, and by Him, then, we know God. Otherwise, and without Scripture, without original sin, without a necessary Mediator, we cannot absolutely prove God, nor teach a good doctrine and sound morals.

But by Jesus Christ and in Jesus Christ, we prove God and teach doctrine and morals. Jesus Christ, then, is the true God of men. Not only do we know God only through Jesus Christ, but we know ourselves only through Jesus Christ ...

Blaise Pascal continued in *Thoughts, Letters and Opuscules*:

We know life, death, only through Jesus Christ. Except by Jesus Christ we know not what life is, what our death is, what God is, what we ourselves are. Thus, without Scripture, which has only Jesus Christ for its object, we know nothing, and we see not only obscurity and confusion in the nature of God, but in nature herself.

Without Jesus Christ, man must be in sin and misery; with Jesus Christ, man is exempt from sin and misery. In Him is all our virtue, and all our felicity. Out of Him, there is nothing but sin, misery, error, darkness, death, and despair.

After Pascal's death, August 19, 1662, a note found among his person effects stated:

"The God of Abraham, the God of Isaac, the God of Jacob," not of philosophers and scholars.

ᴄℛ

GREAT PLAGUE OF LONDON & SIR ISAAC NEWTON

Isaac Newton was born on December 25, 1642, the same year Galileo died. His mother was widowed twice, resulting in him being raised by his grandmother. He was sent off to grammar school and then to Trinity College, Cambridge, 1661.

The City of London was ravaged numerous times by the Plague: 1563, 1593, 1603, 1625, 1636, and 1665. The Great Plague of London 1665–1666 killed over 100,000, a quarter of the city's population, in just 18 months.

Daniel Defoe, author of *Robinson Crusoe*, compiled a chronology "A Journal of the Plague Year." Samuel Pepys described in his diary, June of 1665:

> This day, much against my will, I did in Drury-lane see ... houses marked with a red cross upon the doors, and "Lord have mercy upon us" writ there – which was a sad sight to me, being the first of that kind that to my remembrance I ever saw ... Houses infected by the Plague had to have a red cross one foot high marked on their door and were shut up – often with the victims inside ...

Pepys continued:

> It put me into an ill conception of myself and my smell, so that I was forced to

buy some roll-tobacco to smell and chaw – which took away the apprehension ...

Tobacco was highly prized for its medicinal value, especially against the Plague ... There to my great trouble hear that the plague is come into the City ... which ... troubles me mightily ...

To the office to finish my letters, and then home to bed – being troubled at the sickness, and my head filled also with ... how to put my things and estate in order, in case it should please God to call me away – which God dispose of to his own glory.

The children's nursery rhyme "Ring-o-ring a rosie," has many possible origins postulated, one of which is that it contains an oblique reference to the Plague.

On the heels of the Plague was the Great Fire of London in 1666.

During this time, Issac Newton was studying at Cambridge, but the university shut down as a precaution against the Plague. Being in a sense self-quarantined, he left London for the country. John Conduitt, husband to Newton's niece, wrote:

In the year 1666, Newton retired again from Cambridge to his mother in Lincolnshire.

Whilst he was pensively meandering in a garden it came into his thought that the power of gravity (which brought an apple from a tree to the ground) was not limited to a certain distance from Earth, but that this power must extend much further than was usually thought. "Why not as high as the Moon" said he to himself & if so, that must influence her motion & perhaps retain her orbit, whereupon he fell a calculating what would be the effect of that supposition.

The *Memoirs of Sir Isaac Newton's Life*, written by William Stukeley, gave a similar story:

Why should that apple always descend perpendicularly to the ground, thought he to himself; occasioned by the fall of an apple, as he sat in contemplative mood. Why should it not go sideways, or upwards? But constantly to the Earth's center?

Assuredly the reason is, that the Earth draws it. There must be a drawing power in matter. And the sum of the drawing power in the matter of the Earth must be in the Earth's center, not in any side of the Earth.

Therefore does this apple fall perpendicularly or towards the center? If matter thus draws matter; it must be proportion of its quantity. Therefore the apple draws the Earth, as well as the Earth draws the apple.

Newton became a renowned mathematician and a natural philosopher. He formulated the three laws of motion, which aided in advancement of the discipline of dynamics. He explained in *Mathematical Principles of Natural Philosophy*, 1687:

FIRST LAW: An object either remains at rest or continues to move at a constant velocity, unless acted upon by a force.

SECOND LAW: Force equals mass times acceleration.

THIRD LAW: When one body exerts a force on a second body, the second body simultaneously exerts a force equal in magnitude and opposite in direction on the first body.

Newton's Law of Universal Gravitation is that every particle attracts every other particle with a force that is directly proportional to the product of their masses and inversely proportional to the square of the distance between their centers. He used these laws to explain Kepler's laws of planetary motion.

He broke Aristotle's two-thousand year old dictum that there are two sets of rules: one set for what was on the earth and the other set for what was in the heavens. Newton showed that there was only one set of rules that applies everywhere.

Newton is considered a father of modern science and modern physics. He was honored to occupy the Lucasian Chair of Mathematics, 1669, and was elected Fellow of the Royal Society, 1672. He was given the position of Master of the Mint, 1699, and in 1701, entered Parliament.

In addition to discovering the laws of universal gravitation, Newton was a discoverer of calculus. He helped develop it into a comprehensive branch of mathematics. He constructed one of the first practical reflecting telescopes.

Using a prism, Newton demonstrated that a beam of light contained all the colors of the rainbow. He laid the foundation for the great law of energy conservation and developed the particle theory of light propagation.

In 1703, Sir Issac Newton became the President of the Royal Society, and served in that position until his death.

Contemporaries of Newton during the era of Scientific Revolution were:

- Edmund Halley, English astronomer for whom is named "Halley's Comet";
- Robert Boyle, English chemist;
- Blaise Pascal, French mathematician;
- Christopher Wren, English architect;
- Montesquieu, French philosopher;
- King Louis XIV, Sun King of France;
- Johann Sebastian Bach, German composer;
- Rembrandt, Dutch painter;
- Abel Tasman, Dutch navigator for whom is named "Tasmania";
- John Bunyan, English Baptist author;
- Cotton Mather, Puritan Massachusetts leader;
- William Penn, Quaker Pennsylvania founder;
- Edward Teach, known as the pirate "Blackbeard";
- English Civil War, 1642–1651 and beheading of King Charles I, 1649;
- English Commonwealth under Oliver Cromwell, 1649–1658;
- Richard Cromwell, 1658–1659;
- Restoration of the Monarchy with King Charles II, 1660–1685;
- Reign of King James II, 1685–1688;
- Reign of King William and Queen Mary, 1689–1702;
- Reign of Queen Anne, 1702–1714;
- Reign of King George I, 1714–1727.

Newton wrote one of the most important scientific books ever, *Principia*, 1687, in which he stated:

> This most beautiful system of the sun, planets, and comets, could only proceed from the counsel and dominion of an intelligent and powerful Being ... All variety of created objects which represent order and life in the universe could happen only by the willful reasoning of its original Creator, whom I call the "Lord God" ...

> This Being governs all things, not as the soul of the world, but as Lord over all; and on account of His dominion He is wont to be called "Lord God" ... The supreme God exists necessarily, and by the same necessity He exists always and everywhere.

Newton wrote in the last query of *Optics, or, a Treatise of the Reflections, Refractions, Inflexions and Colours of Light* (1704, London, 1730, 4th edition, quoted in Sullivan, p.125–126):

> Now by the help of these principles, all material things seem to have been composed of the hard and solid particles, above-mentioned, variously associated in the first creation by the counsel of an intelligent agent. For it became him who created them to set them in order. And if he did so, it's unphilosophical to seek for any other origin of the world, or to pretend that it might arise out of a chaos by the mere laws of nature; though being once formed, it may continue by those laws for many ages.

Newton wrote in *Principia*, 1687:

From His true dominion it follows that the true God is a living, intelligent and powerful Being; and from His other perfections, that He is supreme, or most perfect. He is eternal and infinite, omnipotent and omniscient; that is, His duration reaches from eternity to eternity; His presence from infinity to infinity; He governs all things, and knows all things that are or can be done.

Newton was quoted in *Memoirs of the Life, Writings, and Discoveries of Sir Isaac Newton* by Sir David Brewster (Edinburgh, Thomas Constable and Co., 1855, Vol. II, 354):

God made and governs the world invisibly, and has commanded us to love and worship him, and no other God; to honor our parents and masters, and love our neighbors as ourselves; and to be temperate, just, and peaceable, and to be merciful even to brute beasts.

And by the same power by which he gave life at first to every species of animals, he is able to revive the dead, and has revived Jesus Christ our Redeemer, who has gone into the heavens to receive a kingdom, and prepare a place for us, and is next in dignity to God, and may be worshiped as the Lamb of God, and has sent the Holy Ghost to comfort us in his absence, and will at length return and reign over us.

Sir Isaac Newton wrote in *Optics*, 1704:

God in the beginning formed matter in solid, massy, hard, impenetrable, movable particles, of such sizes and figures, and with such other properties, and in such proportion to space, as most conduced to the end for which he formed them.

Sir Isaac Newton devoted more time to the study of Scripture than to science (as cited in *Tiner* 1975):

> I have a fundamental belief in the Bible as the Word of God, written by those who were inspired. I study the Bible daily.

Newton stated:

> We account the Scriptures of God to be the most sublime philosophy. I find more sure marks of authenticity in the Bible than in any profane history whatsoever ... Worshiping God and the Lamb in the temple: God, for his benefaction in creating all things, and the Lamb, for his benefaction in redeeming us with his blood.

Captivated by Bible prophecy, Newton wrote *Observations on the Prophecies of Daniel and the Apocalypse of St. John* (published in 1733), in which he stated:

> Daniel was in the greatest credit amongst the Jews, till the reign of the Roman Emperor Hadrian. And to reject his prophecies, is to reject the Christian religion. For this religion is founded upon his prophecy concerning the Messiah.

He concluded his introductory chapter:

> Daniel is most distinct in order of time, and easiest to be understood, and therefore in those things which relate to the last times, he must be made the key to the rest.

In his *Preface to The Prophecies of Daniel and the Apocalypse* (Published 1733), Sir Isaac Newton quoted a letter to Richard Bentley, dated December 10, 1692:

> When I wrote my treatise about our System I had an eye upon such Principles as

might work with considering men for the belief of a Deity and nothing can rejoice me more than to find it useful for that purpose.

Sir Isaac Newton wrote in *Observations on the Prophecies of Daniel and the Apocalypse of St. John* (published 1733):

> The Book of Revelation exhibits to us the same peculiarities as that of Nature ... The history of the Fall of Man – of the introduction of moral and physical evil, the prediction of the Messiah, the actual advent of our Savior, His instructions, His miracles, His death, His resurrection, and the subsequent propagation of His religion by the unlettered fishermen of Galilee, are each a stumbling-block to the wisdom of this world ...

> But through the system of revealed truth which this Book contains is, like that of the universe, concealed from common observation, yet the labors of the centuries have established its Divine origin, and developed in all its order and beauty the great plan of human restoration.

In *Observations on the Prophecies of Daniel and the Apocalypse of St. John* (published 1733), Sir Isaac Newton wrote:

> The folly of Interpreters has been, to foretell times and things, by this Prophecy, as if God designed to make them Prophets. By this rashness they have not only exposed themselves, but brought the Prophecy also into contempt. The design of God was much otherwise.

He gave this and the Prophecies of the Old Testaments, not to gratify men's curiosities by enabling them to foreknow things, but that after they were fulfilled they might be interpreted by the event; and his own Providence, not the Interpreters, be then manifested thereby to the world.

For the event of things predicted many ages before, will then be a convincing argument that the world is governed by providence.

In *Observations on the Prophecies of Daniel and the Apocalypse of St. John* (published 1733), Newton wrote:

For the prophets and apostles have foretold that as Israel often revolted and brake the covenant, and upon repentance renewed it, so there should be a falling away among the Christians, soon after the days of the Apostles, and that in the latter days God would destroy the impenitent revolters, and make a new covenant with his people.

And the giving ear to the prophets is a fundamental character of the true church … For as the few and obscure Prophecies concerning Christ's first coming were for setting up the Christian religion, which all nations have since corrupted, so the many and clear Prophecies, concerning the things to be done at Christ's second coming, are not only for predicting but also for effecting a recovery and re-establishment of the long-lost truth, and setting up a kingdom wherein dwells righteousness.

The event will prove the Apocalypse, and this Prophecy, thus proved and understood, will open the old Prophets and all together will make known the true religion, and establish it ...

An angel must fly through the midst of heaven with the everlasting Gospel to preach to all nations, before Babylon falls, and the Son of man reaps his harvest. (referencing the Book of Revelation 14:6)

The Encyclopedia of Philosophy described Sir Isaac Newton:

Newton himself was a student of Old Testament prophecies and believed in the Scriptures as inerrant guides.

In his book *Chronology*, Newton studied the sequence of historical events and inserted a geometric diagram of Solomon's Temple, giving the lengths of the Temple in relation to the measurement of time. This was in accordance with the Renaissance view that the Temple was a microcosm of God's creation embodying the order of the universe.

Economist John Maynard Keynes purchased all of Newton's known manuscripts and personal notes at auction. After studying them, John Maynard Keynes wrote of Newton:

He regarded the universe as a cryptogram set by the Almighty, just as he himself wrapped the discovery of calculus in a cryptogram ...

He looked on the whole universe and all that is in it as a riddle, as a secret which could be read by applying pure thought to certain evidence, certain mystic clues which God had laid about the world to allow a sort of philosopher's treasure hunt.

Newton (as cited in *Tiner* 1975):

Atheism is so senseless. When I look at the solar system, I see the earth at the right distance from the sun to receive the proper amounts of heat and light. This did not happen by chance.

Newton wrote in a *Short Scheme of the True Religion* (Sir David Brewster, *Memoirs of the Life, Writings, and Discoveries of Sir Isaac Newton*, Edinburgh, Thomas Constable and Co., 1855, Vol. II, p. 347–348):

Opposite to godliness is atheism in profession, and idolatry in practice. Atheism is so senseless and odious to mankind, that it never had many professors.

Can it be by accident that all birds, beasts, and men have their right side and left side alike shaped, (except in their bowels); and just two eyes, and no more, on either side of the face; and just two ears on either side of the head; and a nose with two holes; and either two forelegs, or two wings, or two arms on the shoulders, and two legs on the hips, and no more?

Whence arises this uniformity in all their outward shapes but from the counsel and contrivance of an Author?

Whence is it that the eyes of all sorts of living creatures are transparent to the very bottom, and the only transparent members in the body, having on the outside a hard transparent skin, and within transparent humours, with a crystalline lens in the middle, and a pupil before the lens, all of them so finely shaped and fitted for vision, that no artist can mend them?

Did blind chance know that there was light, and what was its refraction, and fit the eyes of all creatures, after the most curious manner, to make use of it? These, and suchlike considerations, always have, and ever will prevail with mankind, to believe that there is a Being who made all things, and has all things in his power, and who is therefore to be feared.

We are, therefore, to acknowledge one God, infinite, eternal, omnipresent, omniscient, omnipotent, the Creator of all things, most wise, most just, most good, most holy.

We must love him, fear him, honor him, trust in him, pray to him, give him thanks, praise him, hallow his name, obey his commandments, and set time apart for his service, as we are directed in the Third and Fourth Commandments, for this is the love of God that we keep his commandments, and his commandments are not grievous (I John 5:3).

And these things we must not do to any mediators between him and us, but to him alone, that he may give his angels charge over us, who, being our fellow servants, are pleased with the worship which we give to their God. And this is the first and the principle part of religion. This always was and always will be the religion of all God's people, from the beginning to the end of the world.

Sir Isaac Newton stated:

There is one God, the Father, ever-living, omnipresent, omniscient, almighty, the Maker of heaven and earth, and one Mediator between God and man, the man Christ Jesus ... To us there is but one God, the Father, of whom are all things, and one Lord Jesus Christ, by whom are all things, and we by Him.

That is, we are to worship the Father alone as God Almighty, and Jesus alone as the Lord, the Messiah, the Great King, the Lamb of God who was slain, and hath redeemed us with His blood, and made us kings and priests.

Sir Isaac Newton died March 20, 1727.

He stated (as cited in *The Religion of Sir Isaac Newton*, Frank E. Manuel, editor, London, Oxford University Press, 1974, p. 112):

When you are convinced, be not ashamed to profess the truth. For otherwise you may become a stumbling block to others, and inherit the lot of those rulers of the Jews who believed in Christ, but yet were afraid to confess him lest they should be put out of the synagogue ...

Be not ashamed of the truth, but profess it openly and endeavor to convince your brother also that you may inherit at the resurrection the promise made in Daniel 12:3, that "they who turn many to righteousness shall shine as the stars for ever and ever."

And rejoice if you are counted worthy to suffer in your reputation or any other way for the sake of the Gospel, for then, "great is thy reward!"

☙

SIR WILLIAM HERSCHEL

In 1781, the same year the American Revolution ended, William Herschel discovered the first planet since ancient antiquity. He desired to name the planet Georgium Sidus (George's Star), after King George III.

Others wanted to give it the name of Herschel, as Thomas Jefferson wrote from Paris to John Page, August 20, 1785:

You will find in these the tables for the planet Herschel, as far as the observations hitherto made ... You will see ... that Herschel was ... the first astronomer who discovered it to be a planet.

Born in Germany, November 15, 1738, William Herschel was a musician like his father, who was bandmaster in the Hanoverian guard. He was a contemporary of Beethoven, Haydn, and Mozart.

During the Seven Years War, which in America was called the French and Indian War (1756–1763), William Herschel fled to England. There, he was hired as the first organist at St John the Baptist Church in Halifax, and then organist at the prestigious Octagon Chapel in Bath, eventually writing 24 symphonies.

An album of his music was released in 1995 titled: *Sir William Herschel–Music by the Father of Modern Astronomy*, with the description: "First recordings of the orchestrated chamber works by the celebrated 18th century composer/astronomer."

William Herschel pursued astronomy on the side, building his own telescope to observe, not just the solar system, but "the construction of the heavens." He taught himself how to grind and polish telescopic mirrors, becoming preeminent in that field.

His sister, Caroline Herschel (1750–1848), assisted him, and went on to become a renowned astronomer in her own right as the first professional female astronomer. Caroline Herschel received royal recognition for discovering several comets, one of which was named for her, and for discovering M110, the Andromeda Galaxy's second known companion. A crater on the Moon is named for her.

William Herschel constructed over 400 telescopes, including the largest reflecting telescopes of his day, using them to catalog over 90,000 new stars, as well as nebulae and galaxies. He is most known for his discovery of the planet Uranus on March 13, 1781. It is the 3rd largest planet in our solar system, and the 7th planet from the sun.

Uranus, named after the mythological Greek god of the sky, is basically tied with Neptune for having the coldest atmospheric surface temperature, reaching minus 371 degrees Fahrenheit, resulting in both planets being classified as "ice giants."

After Herschel's discovery of Uranus, King George III granted him a permanent salary as a royal astronomer. The King had him move to Windsor so the Royal Family could look through his telescopes.

Herschel identified double-stars, coined the word "asteroid," meaning star-like, and discovered infrared radiation.

The Scientific Papers of Sir William Herschel (published by the Royal Society in 1912), recorded a diary entry he made after meeting Napoleon in Paris in August of 1802. When French scholar Pierre-Simon LaPlace tried to explain creation as a result of naturalistic causes, Herschel recounted:

> The First Consul (Napoleon) ... asked in a tone of exclamation ... when we were speaking of the extent of the sidereal heavens "and who is the author of all this" ... LaPlace wished to shew that a chain of natural causes would account for the construction ... This the First Consul (Napoleon) rather opposed.

Herschel added:

> Much may be said on the subject; by joining the arguments of both we shall be led to "Nature and Nature's God."

The Royal Society editor wrote in a footnote of Herschel's missing letters:

> Some 400 pages ... are still extant (existing) ... We are informed that Herschel in them interweaves his philosophy and even his musical studies with references of an earnest kind to the Creator as a beneficent Deity, expressing his gratitude and addressing Him in a prayerful spirit.

Herschel was made a Knight of the Royal Guelphic Order by Prince Regent, George IV, in 1816.

Sir William Herschel died in his observatory, August 25, 1822. He was buried in St. Laurence Anglican Church in Slough, England, where a stained-glass "Herschel Window" commemorates his astronomical discoveries, with another window quoting Psalm 8:

> When I consider the heavens, the work of Thy fingers, the moon and the stars, which Thou hast ordained, what is man, that Thou art mindful of him?

A contemporary of Sir William Herschel was the famous English poet, Edward Young (1681–1765), whose poem "Night Thoughts" was published in 1742. The poem became so popular it was translated into French, German, Italian, Spanish, Portuguese, Swedish and Magyar, and quoted throughout Europe and America.

Line 771 of Edward Young's poem "Night Thoughts" is thought to reference Herschel:

> By mortal ear, the glorious Architect,
>
> In this His universal temple hung
>
> With lustres, with innumerable lights,
>
> That shed religion on the soul; at once,
>
> The temple, and the preacher! O how loud
>
> It calls devotion! genuine growth of Night!
>
> Devotion! daughter of Astronomy!
>
> An undevout astronomer is mad.

CR

SIR JOHN HERSCHEL

William Herschel initially encouraged his son, John Frederick Herschel, to enter the ministry. John married Margaret Stewart, the daughter of a Scottish Presbyterian.

When his father died, John took his inheritance and his father's telescope and sailed with his wife to South Africa. There, he cataloged hundreds of new stars and nebulae seen from the southern hemisphere.

He observed double stars, the Great Eruption of the stellar system Eta Carinae, and return of Halley's Comet.

Sir John Herschel wrote in a letter to Charles Babbage (*The Shadow of the Telescope: A Biography of John Herschel* by Günther Buttmann, p. 14):

God knows how ardently I wish I had ten lives.

In a diary entry, November 1855, John Herschel wrote:

What God sends is welcome.

John Herschel is quoted in *The Athenaeum, Journal of English Foreign Literature, Science, and the Fine Arts* (London, June 16, 1838, p. 555), as referring to:

God's great book of nature.

While in South Africa, Herschel read Charles Lyell's *Principles of Geology*: being an attempt to explain the former changes of the Earth's surface, by reference to causes now in operation (1830–1833).

Though Lyell rejected the transmutation of species, his book espoused a novel theory of uniformitarianism, that geological changes in the past happened gradually, in direct contrast to the accepted theory of catastrophism.

Influenced by Lyell's book, John Herschel wrote:

> Time! Time! Time! — we must not impugn (attack) the Scripture chronology, but we must interpret it in accordance with whatever shall appear on fair inquiry to be the truth for there cannot be two truths. And really there is scope enough: for the lives of the Patriarchs may as reasonably be extended to 5000 or 50000 years apiece as the days of Creation to as many thousand millions of years.

While Herschel was in South Africa, the *HMS Beagle* landed at Cape Town, South Africa, on June 3, 1836. A passenger disembarked, the young Charles Darwin, who spent time visiting John Herschel. Herschel's fascination with Lyell's long ages for creation may have influenced Darwin in the development of his theory.

The long ages view was a departure from views held by other famous astronomers, such as Johannes Kepler, who, after writing his book *The Harmony of the World* (1619), stated:

> See, I cast the die, and I write the book. Whether it is to be read by the people of the present or of the future makes no difference: let it await its reader for a hundred

years, if God himself has stood ready for 6,000 years for one to study Him.

Astrophysicist Hugh Ross stated:

The age of the Earth makes no difference with respect to Christ's atoning sacrifice for humanity's sin or to the nature and character of God.

Ross added:

What's true will never contradict what's true. Article 2 of the Belgic Confession, based on Psalm 19, Romans 1, and several other texts, declares that God has given us two reliable revelations: the words of Scripture and the facts of nature. Thus, it would be impossible for the facts of nature ever to contradict the words of the Bible.

During the later part of his life, Sir John Frederick Herschel was one of the most sought after men of science in Britain. He advocated for public education:

... to fit (students) for a higher state of existence, by teaching them those (things) which connect them with their Maker and Redeemer.

Dying on May 12, 1871, he was buried in Westminster Abbey next to Sir Isaac Newton. Sir John Herschel was quoted by Marcel de Serres in *On the Physical Facts in the Bible Compared with the Discoveries of the Modern Sciences* (*The Edinburgh New Philosophical Journal*, 1845, Vol. 38, 260):

All human discoveries seem to be made only for the purpose of confirming more strongly the truths come from on high, and contained in the Sacred Writings.

CR

HOSPITALS: CHRISTIANS PIONEERED CARE FOR SICK

From the beginning of recorded history, millions have died from epidemics. Early recorded plagues include:

• Plague of Pharaoh Akhenaten of Egypt, circa 1350 BC;

• Philistine Plague after capturing the Ark of God (I Samuel 5–6);

• Plague of Athens, circa 430 BC, 100,000 deaths;

• Plague of Antonine, 165 AD, brought back by troops from the Middle East, 5 million deaths.

Some ancient cultures had medical practices, often mixed with superstitions, but it was primarily for the king's family, his military, and wealthy ruling elites.

Healthcare for the poor traces its roots to Christianity. The Syrian Church pioneered medical care in the East, as did the Catholic Church in the West.

The Byzantine Empire's School of Nisibis, founded in the 4th century, sometimes referred to as the world's first university, was a Christian center of scientific and medical learning, located in present-day Turkey.

The Assyrian Christian Bukhtishu family had nine generations of physicians who helped found the great medical academy at Gundeshapur, (5th to 9th centuries), in present-day Iran.

The Assyrian Christian physician, Hunayn ibn-Ishaq, wrote a textbook on ophthalmology in 950 AD which remained the authoritative source until 1800 AD.

In both the East and the West, Christians sought to put into practice the words of Jesus in the parable of the sheep and the goats: "I was sick and you visited me," and "Whatever you have done to the least of my brethren, you have done unto me."

Christians followed the example of the good Samaritan in Jesus' parable, Luke 10:25–37:

> But a Samaritan, as he traveled, came where the man was; and when he saw him, he took pity on him. He went to him and bandaged his wounds, pouring on oil and wine. Then he put the man on his own donkey, brought him to an inn and took care of him. The next day he took out two denarii and gave them to the innkeeper. "Look after him," he said, "and when I return, I will reimburse you for any extra expense you may have."

In the 4th century, under the ministry of St. Jerome, a wealthy Christian widow named St. Fabiola gave money to build a hospital for the poor in Rome and cared for the sick herself.

Around the same time, St. Basil distributed food to the poor of Caesarea, then built a poorhouse, hospice, and a hospital.

In 325 AD, the Council of Nicea directed that every city having a cathedral should also have an infirmary or hospital, as people traveling on pilgrimages would often arrive ill.

The word "hosp" is Latin for "traveler," the root word of: hospital, hospitality, host, hostel, and hotel. Hospitals were staffed by religious orders.

In the 6th century took place the Plague of Justinian, beginning in 541 AD, which killed an estimated 100 million, half of the world's known population.

A physician, St. Sampson the Hospitable, turned his home in Constantinople into a free medical clinic for the poor. When Byzantine Emperor Justinian the Great became ill, he sent for St. Sampson. After recovering, the emperor offered to reward Sampson, who requested help establishing a new hospital for the poor, which continued in Constantinople for 600 years.

This plague weakened the Byzantine Empire, leaving it susceptible in the following century to be invaded by Islamic armies. When Muslim warriors invaded Christian Syria in 634 AD and then conquered Byzantine Christian Jerusalem in 638 AD, the hospitals needed to be defended, giving rise to the order of Knights Hospitaller.

During this time, the Benedictine Order began having every monastery establish an infirmary. The Benedictine Monastery in Salerno, Italy, founded the oldest and most famous medical university in Western Europe. One of the oldest hospitals in the world was founded 660 AD in Paris, the Hôtel-Dieu (hostel of God).

Most universities were started in monasteries and cathedrals, notably: Bologna, Paris, Naples, Toulouse, Oxford.

In 710 AD, Muslim warriors invaded Spain and conquered all the way into France, being stopped at the Battle of Tours in 732 AD, by Charles Martel. Martel's grandson was Charlemagne, who was crowned Holy Roman Emperor. Charlemagne decreed that the hospitals which had fallen into disrepair should be restored.

The Byzantine Emperor Alexis Comnenus I sent a plea to Western Europe for help against the Islamic invasion. Pope Urban called on European kings to respond, which was called the First Crusade. There were nine major crusades in the next 200 years.

The Crusades opened up travel between the Holy Land and Europe. Traders, crusaders, and those who went on pilgrimages sometimes brought illnesses back with them.

In 1217, Paris' hospital, the Hôtel-Dieu, was staffed by a dedicated order of Catholic sisters following the Rule of St. Augustine, and later in 1633, by Sisters of Charity.

In 1331, a plague originated in China, where millions died. It was spread by fleas in caravans traveling the Silk Road, and by rats on ships from the Orient and Middle East. Referred to as the Second Plague Pandemic, it reached Constantinople in 1347.

Christians there cared for the sick following in the example of St. Sampson the Hospitable, who centuries earlier ministered to the poor in his home, then founded one of the first hospitals, funded by the Byzantine Emperor. The Benedictine Order cared for the sick in infirmaries and medical clinics in monasteries.

The Bubonic Plague, or Black Death, reached Italy in 1348. In 1360–1363, it reached London, where it killed 20 percent of the population. In 1369, it killed an additional 15 percent. The death toll in Ireland and British Isles was close to 3 million.

In total, the Bubonic Plague killed an estimated 75 to 200 million across Europe. So many died that crops were left standing in fields as there was no one to harvest them.

Often there was no one to bury the dead, so an order of Catholic men formed, called "Alexian Brothers," who collected the bodies of the dead and gave them a Christian burial.

Alexian Brothers also provided hospice care to the dying who were banished from cities. Tragically, there were numerous recurrences of plagues:

- Venice had 22 outbreaks of plague from 1361 to 1528, with its plague of 1576–1577 killing 50,000, a third of its population;
- Plague in Paris (1466), killing 40,000;
- Plague of London in 1563;
- Plague of San Cristóbal de La Laguna (1582–1583), killing 9,000, half the population;
- Plague of London in 1592 and 1603;
- Plague in France (1628–1631), according to historian Geoffrey Parker: "France alone lost almost a million people to plague";
- Amsterdam's plagues of 1623–1625, 1635–1636, 1655, and 1664, killed 10 percent of its population;
- Italian Plague (1629–1631), killing 280,000;
- Andalusia Plague (1637), killing 20,000;
- Plague of Seville (1647–1652), killing 30,000;
- Plague of Naples (1656), killed 150,000, half of the city's population;
- Great Plague of London 1665–1666, which killed 100,000, a fifth of the population.

- Plague of Vienna (1679), killing 76,000;
- Plague of Marseille (1720–1722), killing 200,000;
- Plague of Balkans & Eastern Europe (1738), killing 50,000;
- Plague of Russia (1654) killing 700,000, and (1770–1772), killing nearly 100,000;
- Plague of Persia (1772), killing 2 million.

Jewish populations had higher survival rates because they followed Mosaic instructions of washing, waste disposal, and the isolation of infected individuals for forty days. The Italian word for forty is "quaranta," from which the word "quarantine" is derived.

When the Islamic Turkish Sultan conquered Constantinople in 1453, it ended Europe's trade with India and China along the Silk Road. Europeans sought a sea route, and Columbus set sail, running into what he thought was India, so he name the people he met "Indians." Beginning in 1545, the Cocoliztli Plague began in Mexico, killing an estimated 15 million.

In 1650, a malaria plague occurred in South America.

In 1633, Paris' Hôtel-Dieu began to be staffed by another order of nuns, the Sisters of Charity. They went on to establish hospitals and schools for the poor across all of France.

In this era, wealthy families had doctors visit them at their homes, but the poor were primarily cared for at Catholic hospitals.

Other Catholic religious orders, such as the Trinitarians, collected alms and sailed to North Africa to ransom Europeans who had been kidnapped and sold into Muslim slavery.

In 1605, St. Vincent de Paul was sailing from Marseille, France, when he was captured by Muslim Barbary pirates and sold into slavery in Tunis, North Africa. After two years, he was able to convert one of his master's wives to Christianity, and then his master. In 1607, he escaped back to Europe, and started religious orders to care for the poor in hospitals.

By 1789, there were 426 hospitals in France run by 6,000 Sisters of Charity. They also founded hospitals in countries across Europe, including Poland, Austria, Switzerland, Italy, Spain, and Silesia.

A New Testament verse inspiring the nuns was I Timothy 5:9–10:

> ... a widow be taken into the number ... well reported of for good works ... if she have lodged strangers, if she have washed the saints' feet, if she have relieved the afflicted, if she have diligently followed every good work.

During France's Revolution and its Reign of Terror, mobs broke into the mother house of the Sisters of Charity. The authorities demanded the nuns deny their faith and submit to the new atheistic secular government. When they chose to keep their faith, the government rounded them up and shot them.

Another group of nuns, known as the Martyrs of Compiègne, sang a hymn as one by one they were led up the scaffold and beheaded with the guillotine on July 17. 1794.

In 1793, France's new anti-Christian government tried to disband religious orders, such as the Sisters of Charity, which cared for the poor. In response, the Sisters of Charity spread healthcare for the poor across the world.

In the 19th century, they began hospitals in: Portugal, Hungary, England, Scotland, Ireland, North and South America, Turkey, Syria, Egypt, Persia, Abyssinia, China and Jerusalem.

Geoffrey Blainey wrote in *A Short History of Christianity* (Penguin Viking; 2011, p. 214):

(The Catholic Church) conducted hospitals for the old and orphanages for the young; hospices for the sick of all ages; places for the lepers; and hostels or inns where pilgrims could buy a cheap bed and meal. It supplied food to the population during famine and distributed food to the poor.

More Catholic religious orders were formed to care for the sick, nurse the ill, change bed pans, and start leper colonies, such as: Daughters of Charity of Saint Vincent de Paul (founded 1633); and Sisters of St. Joseph (founded 1650).

Beginning in the early 1800s, with the Second Great Awakening and the Industrial Revolution, hospitals were also founded by Protestant Christian denominations, most notably: Seventh Day Adventists, Baptists, Episcopalians, Lutherans, Methodists, and Presbyterians.

Whereas Catholic healthcare began with the focus of preparing a person's soul for death when they would meet God in "the hereafter," Protestant healthcare focused more on "the here and now," being motivated to clean up the slums in crowded cities and send medical missionaries to undeveloped countries.

America experienced plagues of yellow fever, bubonic plague, influenza, smallpox, measles, chickenpox, and typhus. These often began in crowded cities, such as in New England, 1616, 1633, 1713, 1721, 1732, 1747, and 1788.

Thousands of deaths occurred in the crowded port city of Boston, then spread to other cities. Sick were often buried in mass graves. Native Indian populations were decimated.

America's first hospital was Pennsylvania Hospital founded in 1751 by Dr. Thomas Bond and Benjamin Franklin "to care for the sick-poor and insane who were wandering the streets of Philadelphia."

The Hospital cornerstone recorded text composed by Franklin:

> In the year of Christ, 1755 ... This building, by the bounty of the Government and of many private persons, was piously founded, for the relief of the sick and miserable. May the God of mercies bless the undertaking!

In *Some Account of the Pennsylvania Hospital from its first rise (in 1751), to the beginning of the fifth month, called May 1754,* Benjamin Franklin stated:

> It would be a neglect of that justice which is due to the physicians and surgeons of this hospital, not to acknowledge that their care and skill, and their punctual and regular attendance, under the Divine Blessing, has been a principal means of advancing this charity to the flourishing state in which we have now the pleasure to view it. Relying on the continuance of the Favour of Heaven, upon the future endeavors of all who may be concerned in the management of the institution, for its further advancement, we close this account with the abstract of a sermon, preached before the Governors.

The second oldest hospital in America was New York Presbyterian Hospital founded in 1771, founded by Samuel Bard, who was a personal physician to George Washington.

※

SMALLPOX DURING THE REVOLUTION

During the Revolutionary War, John Adams wrote to his wife Abigail, April 13, 1777:

> Disease has destroyed ten men for us, where the sword of the enemy has killed one.

Soldiers camped in close quarters came down with typhoid, yellow fever, and particularly, smallpox, of which an estimated 30 percent of soldiers became infected.

Though the New England colonies had experienced occurrences of the disease, thought to have been brought by travelers from the Caribbean, a major smallpox epidemic began in 1775 when the British evacuated Boston, which they had occupied for 9 months, and left their infected soldiers behind.

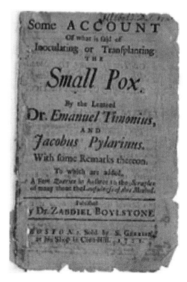

Spread only by direct human contact, in the next seven years, smallpox dispersed from Boston across the continent, reaching as far away as New Orleans, Mexico, areas of Texas, and the Great Plains.

Smallpox killed an estimated 145,000 settlers and Indians.

The migrating Shoshone are thought to have carried it to the Pueblos territory of New Mexico. It showed up in tribes of the Pacific Northwest, in the Canadian interior at trading posts of the Hudson's Bay Company, and even in Alaska.

Fortunately for George Washington, he was immune to smallpox as he had contracted it at the age of 19 when he traveled to Barbados with his older half-brother Lawrence in 1751.

On July 4, 1775, Washington cautioned against travel around Boston:

> ... as there may be danger of introducing smallpox into the army.

Churches and homes were used as hospitals.

On July 20, 1775, Washington wrote to Congress, that he had:

> ... been particularly attentive to the least symptoms of the smallpox ... We shall continue the utmost vigilance against this most dangerous enemy.

Washington directed Lieut. Col. Loammi Baldwin to prevent officers from meeting:

> ... with the people who ... came out of Boston ... There is great reason to suspect that the smallpox is amongst them, which every precaution must be used to prevent its spreading.

In November of 1775, Washington noted:

> ... smallpox is now in Boston, I have used the precaution of prohibiting such as lately came out from coming near our camp.

On December 15, 1775, Washington explained to Joseph Reed that:

> ... smallpox is in every part of Boston ... a surety against any attempt of ours to attack. If we escape the smallpox in this camp ... it will be miraculous. Every precaution that can be is taken to guard against this evil.

On December 4, 1775, Washington informed Congress that the British were sending civilians infected with smallpox out of the city:

By recent information ... General Howe is going to send out a number of the inhabitants ... A sailor says that a number of these coming out have been inoculated with the design of spreading the smallpox through this ... camp.

As a preventative measure, a weakened strain of the disease would be introduced into a healthy person's body allowing them to build up an immunity.

Many of the Continental Army officers' wives decided to be inoculated with smallpox. On May 23, 1776, Martha Washington was inoculated by a doctor in Philadelphia.

The method of preventative inoculation varied from scrapping a dried scab into fine powder, then blowing it up a person's nose, to more invasive procedures.

John Adams described in a letter to his wife the crude inoculation he endured in July of 1764:

Dr. Perkins demanded my left arm ... They took their lancets and with their points divided the skin about a quarter of an inch and just suffering the blood to appear, buried a thread (infected) about a quarter of an inch long in the channel.

A little lint was then laid over the scratch and a piece of rag pressed on, and then a bandage bound over all, and I was bid go where and do what I pleased ...

Do not conclude from any thing I have written that I think inoculation a light matter – A long and total abstinence from everything in nature that has any taste; two long heavy vomits, one heavy cathartic (to purge bowels), four and twenty mercurial and antimonial pills, and, three weeks of close confinement to an house, are, according to my estimation, no small matters.

On January 1, 1777, British ships sailing under the flag of truce released 200 American prisoners at Connecticut's Milford Harbor – all suffering from smallpox.

Within a month, 46 had died along with one of their caregivers, Captain Stephen Stow. British officer Robert Donkin had suggested, as cited in a book published in 1777:

Dip arrows in matter of smallpox, and twang them at the American rebels … This would … disband these stubborn, ignorant, enthusiastic savages.

Quebec might have been captured by Americans in December of 1775, which would have possibly resulted in Canada becoming part of the United States, had it not been for smallpox.

American Captain Hector McNeal told a Congressional Committee investigating the failure of the army's expedition to Canada:

Smallpox was sent out of Quebec by (British) Governor Guy Carleton, inoculating the poor people at government expense for the purpose of giving it to our army.

General Benedict Arnold reported that nearly 1,200 American troops at Montreal were also suffering from smallpox:

From the 1st of January to the 1st of March, we have never had more than seven hundred effective men on the ground, and frequently not more than five hundred. Washington quoted from a letter by General Sullivan that:

The army is sickly, many with the smallpox, and he is apprehensive the militia ordered to join them will not escape the infection.

General Gates conceded:

As fine an Army as has ever marched into Canada has this year been entirely ruined with smallpox. The line of retreat extended near 13 miles distance and a great part of them sick with smallpox.

John Adams wrote from Philadelphia, June of 1776:

Our misfortunes in Canada are enough to melt a heart of stone. The smallpox is ten times more terrible than Britons, Canadians, and Indians together. This was the cause of our precipitate retreat from Quebec.

George Washington wrote his concerns regarding inoculating his troops:

Should we inoculate generally, the enemy, knowing it, will certainly take advantage of our situation.

The threat of smallpox did not lessen until widespread inoculations were called for by Dr. Benjamin Rush,

CR

DR. BENJAMIN RUSH

Dr. Benjamin Rush was born January 4, 1745. He was a surgeon general of the middle department of the Continental Army, tending to wounded soldiers during the Battle of Princeton, including General Hugh Mercer.

He inoculated Virginia Governor Patrick Henry against smallpox, as well as Pennsylvania troops, resulting in their low rate of illness.

Benjamin Rush had studied medicine in Philadelphia, then in Europe under the world's foremost physicians, and then returned to Philadelphia in 1769.

Though some of his practices are archaic by today's standards, he is considered the "Father of American Medicine" for his work on staff at the Pennsylvania Hospital, where he opened the first free medical clinic.

Dr. Rush was among the first to recognize alcoholism as a disease and began to promote temperance. He wrote the first textbook on mental illness and psychiatry, recommending treatment with kindness, earning him the title "Father of American Psychiatry."

He was a member of the Continental Congress and signed the Declaration of Independence. His wife was Julia, was the daughter of Richard Stockton, also a signer of the Declaration of Independence.

Thomas Paine consulted with Dr. Benjamin Rush when writing his stirring pamphlet *Common Sense*. Rush helped write Pennsylvania's Constitution and was as a member of the Pennsylvania State Convention which ratified the U.S. Constitution in 1787.

He was Treasurer of the U.S. Mint. He helped found Dickinson College to train physicians, and the Philadelphia Dispensary. A statue of Dr. Benjamin Rush stands on the campus of Dickinson College.

During the dread summer of 1793, Dr. Rush stayed in Philadelphia battling the disease of Yellow Fever which killed thousands. He was the first to recognize that yellow fever was not contagious, leading to the later discovery that it was spread by mosquito bites.

He supported ending slavery prior to the Revolution, forming a Society for the Abolition of Slavery. He founded a Sunday School Union and the Philadelphia Bible Society.

Perhaps Rush's most beloved contribution to American history was in 1812 encouraging John Adams to write to Thomas Jefferson, breaking the silence which had existed between them for years due to earlier political differences.

A proponent of public education for young women as well as men, Rush wrote his *Thoughts Upon the Mode of Education Proper in a Republic*, 1786:

> I proceed ... to inquire what mode of education we shall adopt so as to secure to the state all of the advantages that are to be derived from the proper instruction of the youth; and here I beg leave to remark that the only foundation for a useful education in a republic is to be laid on the foundation of religion.

Without this there can be no virtue, and without virtue there can be no liberty, and liberty is the object and life of all republican governments.

But the religion I mean to recommend in this place is that of the New Testament ... Its doctrines and precepts are calculated to promote the happiness of society and the safety and well-being of civil government.

Dr. Benjamin Rush wrote in *A Plan for Free Schools*, 1787:

Let the children ... be carefully instructed in the principles and obligations of the Christian religion. This is the most essential part of education.

Rush wrote to Jeremy Belknap, July 13, 1789:

The great enemy of the salvation of man, in my opinion, never invented a more effectual means of extirpating (removing) Christianity from the world than by persuading mankind that it was improper to read the Bible at schools.

Dr. Benjamin Rush wrote in an essay, "A Defense of the Use of the Bible as a School Book," included in his 1798 work, *Essays, Literary, Moral and Philosophical*:

The Bible, when not read in schools, is seldom read in any subsequent period of life ... It should be read in our schools in preference to all other books from its containing the greatest portion of that kind of knowledge which is calculated to produce private and public temporal happiness.

He wrote in *Essays, Literary, Moral, and Philosophical*, 1798:

I know there is an objection among many people to teaching children doctrines of any kind, because they are liable to be controverted. But let us not be wiser than our Maker. If moral precepts alone could have reformed mankind, the mission of the Son of God into all the world would have been unnecessary.

The perfect morality of the Gospel rests upon the doctrine which, though often controverted has never been refuted: I mean the vicarious life and death of the Son of God.

"Vicarious" is defined in *Merriam–Webster's Dictionary* as: "suffered by one person as a substitute for another or to the benefit or advantage of another: substitutionary."

Dr. Rush stated:

Without religion, I believe that learning does real mischief to the morals and principles of mankind.

He wrote his *Thoughts Upon the Mode of Education Proper in a Republic*, 1786:

A Christian cannot fail of being a republican ... for every precept of the Gospel inculcates those degrees of humility, self-denial, and brotherly kindness which are directly opposed to the pride of monarchy ... A Christian cannot fail of being useful to the republic, for his religion teaches him that no man "liveth to himself." And lastly a Christian cannot fail of being wholly inoffensive, for his religion teaches him in all things to do to others what he would wish, in like circumstances, they should do to him.

Dr. Benjamin Rush explained in *Essays, Literary, Moral, and Philosophical*, 1798:

Christianity is the only true and perfect religion, and that in proportion as mankind adopts its principles and obeys its precepts, they will be wise and happy ...

In contemplating the political institutions of the United States, I lament that we waste so much time and money in punishing crimes and take so little pains to prevent them. We profess to be republicans, and yet we neglect the only means of establishing and perpetuating our republican forms of government, that is, the universal education of our youth in the principles of Christianity by the means of the Bible.

For this Divine book, above all others, favors that equality among mankind, that respect for just laws, and those sober and frugal virtues, which constitute the soul of republicanism.

On July 9, 1788, Rush wrote to Elias Boudinot regarding a parade in Philadelphia:

The Rabbi of the Jews locked arms of two ministers of the Gospel was a most delightful sight. There could not have been a more happy emblem.

Dr. Benjamin Rush wrote:

I have been alternately called an Aristocrat and a Democrat. I am neither. I am a Christocrat. I believe all power ... will always fail of producing order and happiness in the hands of man. HE alone who created and redeemed man is qualified to govern him.

Rush died in Philadelphia on April 19, 1813, and was buried in the yard of Christ's Church. Memorials to him stand on Navy Hill in Washington, D.C., and near the Harvard Square Library. John Adams wrote:

Another of our friends of seventy-six is gone, my dear Sir, another of the co-signers of the Independence of our country ... A better man than Rush could not have left us, more benevolent, more learned, of finer genius, or more honest. I know of no Character living or dead who has done more real good in America.

During his final illness, Dr. Benjamin Rush wrote to his wife:

My excellent wife, I must leave you, but God will take care of you.

By the mystery of Thy holy incarnation;

by Thy holy nativity;

by Thy baptism, fasting, and temptation;

by Thine agony and bloody sweat;

by Thy cross and passion;

by Thy precious death and burial;

by Thy glorious resurrection and ascension, and

by the coming of the Holy Ghost, blessed Jesus, wash away all my impurities, and receive me into Thy everlasting kingdom.

ℭℜ

HEALTHCARE IN AMERICA

In 1793, a Yellow Fever outbreak resulted in 5,000 deaths in Philadelphia, followed by 25 different outbreaks across the country over the next century, possibly brought by slaves or merchants from Africa or Caribbean and spread by mosquitoes.

In 1811, the third oldest hospital in America was founded, the Massachusetts General Hospital, being significantly financed by Jewish residents Moses Michael Hays, a neighbor of Paul Revere, and Abraham and Judah Touro.

At the time of the Revolutionary War, the United States had a population of 3 million, which was: 98 percent Protestant, 1 percent Catholic, 1/10th of 1 percent Jewish.

In 1809, Mother Elizabeth Ann Seton brought the Sisters of Charity to the United States. Beginning in 1829, Sisters who immigrated largely from France and Ireland founded 299 hospitals in America in the 19th century, including: Mayo Clinic, St. Vincent's, Baltimore Infirmary, and hospitals for the working classes in Buffalo, Philadelphia and Boston.

More Catholic religious orders were formed for the purpose of caring for the sick:

- Sisters of Mercy, founded 1827;
- Little Sisters of the Poor, founded 1839;
- Sisters of Providence, founded 1843;
- Sisters of Charity of St. Augustine, founded 1851;
- Fr. Damien's colony for lepers at Molokai, Hawaii, founded 1864. A statue of him is at Hawaii's Capitol and in the U.S. Capitol;
- Sisters of St. Mary, founded 1872;
- Sisters of the Little Company of Mary, founded 1877; and
- Sisters of the Sorrowful Mother, founded 1883.

In an era when most women had family obligations and could only volunteer temporarily as battlefield nurses, the sisters were systematically trained in nursing skills and serve sacrificially their entire lives.

Nursing pioneer Florence Nightingale, who cared for the British troops during the Crimean War, 1853–1856, once said: "What training is there to compare with that of a Catholic nun." The nuns' habit developed into the nurses' outfit with its distinctive cap.

In 1830, Sisters of Charity established the first hospital west of the Mississippi River in St. Louis, Missouri. When St. Louis suffered devastating cholera epidemics in 1832 and 1849, which killed thousands, the sisters risked death caring for diseased patients, as described by Bishop Rosati:

> Patients were visited by us day and night with the greatest alacrity and without any fear of death.

Four Daughters of Charity died.

In 1832 there was worldwide Cholera epidemics in which millions died. Cholera originated in India, where the religious practice of some was to bath in the sewage-filled Ganges River.

When the British colonized India, people infected with Cholera brought it back to Europe, killing tens of millions in crowded cities in: England, Ireland, Belgium, Netherlands, France, Spain, Italy, Germany, Hungary, China, Japan, Java, Korea, the Philippines, India, Bengal, Iran, Iraq, Algeria, Tunisia, Egypt, Arabia, and Africa.

Immigrants brought it to America, Canada, Mexico, Venezuela, Brazil, and the Pacific Coast.

U.S. Senator Henry Clay asked for a Joint Resolution of Congress to request that President Jackson set: "A Day of Public Humiliation, Prayer and Fasting to be observed by the people of the United States with religious solemnity."

Beginning in 1845, the Great Irish Potato Famine resulted in an enormous wave of immigration, raising the Catholic population in America to over 20 percent.

In 1848, another wave of Cholera came to America: 5,000 died in New York, with a mass grave on Randall's Island in the East River; 8,000 died in Cincinnati and 3,000 killed in New Orleans.

Spreading up the Mississippi, 5,000 died in St. Louis, a 6% of the city's population and 3,500 in Chicago. Ohio had to postpone its first State Fair.

Settlers spread it along the Oregon Trail to the Pacific Northwest and the Mormon Trail to Utah, and on their way to California Gold Rush.

Indian tribes were devastated.

An estimated 150,000 died in America of Cholera, causing President Zachary Taylor to proclaim a National Day of Fasting in 1849:

> A fearful pestilence which is spreading itself throughout the land ... It is fitting that a people whose reliance has ever been in His protection should humble themselves before His throne ... acknowledging past transgressions ... ask a continuance of the Divine mercy ... and to implore the Almighty ... to stay the destroying hand.

That same year, 1849, English physician John Snow observed that cases of cholera occurred close to a well in Soho neighborhood. This led to his discovery that the disease was spread through contaminated drinking water (*Medical Times and Gazette*; essay on the "Mode of Communication of Cholera"):

> On proceeding to the spot, I found that nearly all the deaths had taken place within a short distance of the (Broad Street) pump ... The result of the inquiry, then,

is, that there has been no particular outbreak or prevalence of cholera in this part of London except among the persons who were in the habit of drinking the water of the above-mentioned pump well ... In consequence of what I said, the handle of the pump was removed on the following day.

Nobel Prize recipient bacteriologist Robert Koch traveled to Egypt and India in 1884 and confirmed the identity of the cholera bacillus which aided in treatment and prevention.

In 1858, there was a Scarlet Fever epidemic in America in which over 20,000, mostly children, died.

During the Civil War, at President Lincoln request, nearly 200 Sisters of Charity served on battlefields and in military hospitals. Just as Clara Barton, founder to the American Red Cross, had volunteered and cared for troops during the Civil War, so did eight different orders of Catholic nuns, numbering over 600 and comprising over a fifth of all female nurses.

A monument was erected in Washington, D.C., to the "Nursing Nuns of the Battlefield," with the inscription:

They comforted the dying, nursed the wounded, carried hope to the imprisoned, gave in His Name a drink of water to the thirsty. To the memory and in honor of the various orders of sisters who gave their services as nurses on battlefields and in hospitals during the Civil War. Erected by the ladies Auxiliary to the Ancient Order of Hibernians of America. A.D. 1924. By Authority of the Congress of the United States.

During the Civil War, U.S. Surgeon General Hammond reported to President

Lincoln that volunteer nurses "cannot compare in efficiency and faithfulness with the Sisters of Charity."

In 1866, another Cholera swept the world. From 1865 to 1906, thousands died from Typhoid epidemics, with over 100,000 during Civil War and Spanish America War; From 1890 to 1900, 100,000 died a year from Tuberculosis.

Over 250 Sisters of Charity served during the Spanish–American War of 1898, where diarrhea, dysentery, typhoid fever, and malaria killed more soldiers than combat.

Georgetown Hospital was founded in 1898 as part of Georgetown University, founded January 23, 1789, by John Carroll, America's first Catholic Bishop. He wrote:

> Freedom and independence, acquired by ... the mingled blood of Protestant and Catholic fellow-citizens, should be equally enjoyed by all.

His cousin was Charles Carroll, the only Catholic to sign the Declaration of Independence, the longest living of the signers, and the wealthiest man in America at the time of the founding.

Charles Carroll paid for the building of a large house for his son, which was later donated to be the main campus of Johns Hopkins University, with its world-renown Schools of Nursing and Medicine.

Dr. Ben Carson, U.S. Secretary of Housing and Urban Development, was Director of Pediatric Neurosurgery at Johns Hopkins Hospital from 1984 until his retirement in 2013.

George Washington ended his letter to Bishop John Carroll:

> May the members of your society in America, animated alone by the pure spirit of Christianity, and still conducting themselves as the faithful subjects of our free government, enjoy every temporal and spiritual felicity. And I presume that your fellow-citizens will not forget the patriotic part which you took in the accomplishment of their Revolution, and the establishment of their government.

During the 1800's, numerous persecutions and pogroms against Jews took place in Europe, Russia, and the Middle East. Many Jewish immigrants fled and came to America. Jewish citizens founded Beth Israel Hospitals in: New York's Lower East Side, 1890; Newark, 1901; and Boston, 1916.

Other illnesses swept the country.

The Spanish Flu began in 1918 during World War I and killed 75 million worldwide.

Throughout the 1920s, there were 200,000 Diphtheria cases a year.

From 1916 to 1952, Polio left millions paralytic, peaking with 60,000 children in 1952.

In 1957, the Asian Flu caused 2 million deaths worldwide. In 1968, the Hong Kong Flu left 1 million dead. From 1960 to the present, AIDS, 30 million deaths worldwide, particularly Africa. In 2020, worldwide 1.4 million have been classified as Covid 19 related deaths.

The Catholic Church went on to have the largest membership of any denomination in America, and it also became the nation's largest medical care provider, with over 600 hospitals and 500 long-term health care facilities.

As of 2018, 10 of the 25 largest healthcare networks in the U.S. were Church affiliated:

- Catholic Health Initiatives–78 hospitals;
- Ascension Health–67 hospitals–Daughters of Charity, Sisters of St. Joseph;
- Trinity Health–44 hospitals, 379 Clinics, Catholic Health Ministries;
- Catholic Healthcare West–41 hospitals, Sisters of Mercy;
- Catholic Health East–34 hospitals, 9 religious congregations & Hope Ministries;
- Catholic Healthcare Partners–33 hospitals, Sisters of Mercy, Daughters of Charity;
- Providence Health & Services–26 hospitals, Sisters of Providence, Sisters of the Little Company of Mary;
- Marian Health System–25 hospitals, Sisters of the Sorrowful Mother.

Inspired by Biblical passages to be charitable, wealthy individuals donated and provided for hospitals in their wills. Catholics, Protestants and Jews pioneered free healthcare for the poor "uninsurable" because they were motivated by Judeo-Christian religious convictions.

The New York Times wrote, August 20, 2011, that Catholic nuns were trained to "see Jesus in the face of every patient."

Mother Teresa reaffirmed this with the Sisters of the Missionaries of Charity being dedicated to: "Wholehearted and Free service to the poorest of the poor." They began by gathering the sick from the gutters in India, and bathing them, clothing them, and

20

ministering to their needs. Mother Teresa stated:

> I see Jesus in every human being. I say to myself, this is hungry Jesus, I must feed him. This is sick Jesus. This one has leprosy or gangrene; I must wash him and tend to him. I serve because I love Jesus.

All physicians originally took a version of the Hippocratic Oath, in which medical skills would not be used to euthanize a patient or commit an abortion:

> I will give no deadly medicine to anyone ... furthermore, I will not give to a woman an instrument to produce an abortion.

Modern revisions of the oath have not only removed these values but removed a physician's freedom of conscience to not participate in them.

It is ironic that in the encroachment of government and for-profit corporations into healthcare, the Judeo-Christian values which pioneered medical care for the poor and needy are being marginalized.

When concerns were brought up during the debates of the Patient Protection and Affordable Care Act, Speaker of the House Nancy Pelosi rushed the legislation to a vote, stating March 9, 2010: "We have to pass the bill so that you can find out what is in it."

"What was in it" were regulations which, in numerous instances, resulted in the government pressuring religiously motivated healthcare professionals to abandon their consciences, as well as the very spiritual beliefs which gave birth to healthcare in the first place.

Similar to the time of the French Revolution, the Christian religious convictions which motivated people of faith to selflessly provide free healthcare for the poor for over a thousand years are now being relegated to insignificance by utilitarian central planners.

President Trump declared January 22, 2018, as National Sanctity of Human Life Day:

> Reverence for every human life, one of the values for which our Founding Fathers fought, defines the character of our Nation. Today, it moves us to promote the health of pregnant mothers and their unborn children ... Medical advances give us an even greater appreciation for the humanity of the unborn.
>
> Today, citizens throughout our great country are working for the cause of life and fighting for the unborn, driven by love and supported by both science and philosophy. These compassionate Americans are volunteers who assist women through difficult pregnancies, facilitate adoptions, and offer hope to those considering or recovering from abortions.
>
> They are medical providers who, often at the risk of their livelihood, conscientiously refuse to participate in abortions ... Thankfully, the number of abortions, which has been in steady decline since 1980, is now at a historic low."

On May 21, 2012, the Archdiocese of New York filed a historic Federal lawsuit against the HHS mandate:

> In order to protect our religious liberties from unwarranted and unprecedented government intrusion, the Archdiocese of New York has filed suit in federal court today seeking to block the recent Health and Human Services mandate that

unconstitutionally attempts to define the nature of the Church's religious ministry and would force religious employers to violate their consciences.

Cardinal Timothy Dolan, Archbishop of New York, October 29, 2012, responded to President Obama's HHS healthcare mandates:

> It is not just about sterilization, abortifacients, and chemical contraception... It's about religious freedom, the sacred right, protected by our constitution ...

Cardinal Dolan, as President of the United States Conference of Catholic Bishops (USCCB), 2010–2013, continued:

> President Obama announced ... the choking mandates from HHS would remain – a shock to me, since he had personally assured me that he would do nothing to impede the good work of the Church ... that he considered the protection of conscience a sacred duty ...
>
> There was still no resolution about the handcuffs placed upon ... Catholic charitable agencies ... just because they will not refer victims of human trafficking, immigrants and refugees, and the hungry of the world, for abortions, sterilization, or contraception.

The United States Conference of Catholic Bishops stated October 12, 2012, regarding a supposed "exemption" to the HHS mandate:

> Last night, the ... statement was made during the Vice Presidential debate regarding the decision of the U.S. Department of Health and Human Services (HHS) to force

virtually all employers to include sterilization and contraception, including drugs that may cause abortion, in the health insurance coverage they provide their employees ...

That exemption ... does not extend to "Catholic social services, Georgetown Hospital" ... or any other religious charity.

On August 15, 1993, Pope John Paul II addressed over 375,000 at Cherry Creek State Park, Colorado, with Vice-President Al Gore in attendance:

At no other time in history, the "culture of death" has assumed a social and institutional form of legality to justify the most horrible crimes against humanity ... massive taking of lives of human beings even before they are born ... Any reference to a "law" guaranteed by the Creator is absent ...

No longer is anything considered intrinsically "good" and "universally binding" ... Vast sectors of society are confused about what is right and what is wrong and are at the mercy of those with the power to "create" opinion and impose it on others ..."

Pope John Paul continued:

The family especially is under attack ... The weakest members of society are the most at risk. The unborn, children, the sick, the handicapped, the old ... Do not be afraid to go out on the streets and into public places ... This is no time to be ashamed of the Gospel. It is a time to preach it from the rooftops ... You must feel the full urgency of the task. Woe to you if you do not succeed in defending life.

ॐ

BENJAMIN FRANKLIN:
PRINTER, INVENTOR, ABOLITIONIST

Ben Franklin was a printer, an ambassador, an author, an inventor, a scientist, and a Founding Father. He was born in Boston, January 17, 1706, the 15th of 18 children, to Josiah Franklin, a poor Puritan candle and soap maker, and dyer of cloth.

At age 12, Benjamin was apprenticed to his brother James Franklin's print shop in Boston. In 1721, Boston experienced its worst smallpox epidemic. James Franklin founded what is considered the first truly independent newspaper in the colonies: *The New-England Courant.*

James formed The Hell–Fire Club and in 1722 published unflattering articles about the Massachusetts governor, resulting in him being arrested and jailed for four weeks.

Benjamin continued to run the paper, publishing articles under the pseudonym "Mrs. Silence Dogood," whom he had quote the Roman poet Cato:

Without freedom of thought there can be no such thing as wisdom, and no such thing as public liberty without freedom of speech.

When James found out the identity of "Mrs. Silence Dogood" was none other than his younger brother, they had a falling out.

At age 17, Benjamin ran away, leaving his apprenticeship without permission, which was illegal and made him a fugitive. Later in life, the brothers reconciled, with Benjamin even providing an apprenticeship for James' son, James, Jr.

In 1723, Franklin arrived in Philadelphia and worked at several print shops.

He soon met Deborah Read. They fell in love and he proposed in 1724, but her mother refused to let them marry due to his unstable financial situation.

Franklin left for Europe, being promised support from Pennsylvania Governor Sir William Keith, which soon failed. While in London, Franklin worked as a typesetter at a print shop near the Church of St. Bartholomew the Great.

In the meantime, Deborah Read's mother had her marry John Rogers, a sweet-talking ne'er-do-well, who could not hold a job. Four months after the wedding, they found out he had another wife in London. Rogers spent all of Deborah's dowry, incurred more debt, ran off the British West Indies where he was killed in a fight.

In 1726, Franklin returned to Philadelphia and renewed his relationship with Deborah. He proposed, but they could not legally marry, as the colony would not grant a divorce based on Rogers' desertion, and they could not prove that Rogers was dead, so Franklin and Deborah had a private ceremony and a common-law marriage.

In 1729, at the age of 23, he began publishing the *Pennsylvania Gazette,* where he designed some of the very first political cartoons.

In 1732, he began publishing *Poor Richard's Almanack*, which sold 10,000 copies a year. Franklin retired at age 42, taught himself five languages, then invented:

- the rocking chair;
- Franklin stove;
- bifocal glasses;
- swim fins;
- a catheter;
- odometer, for measuring postal routes;
- "glass armonica" musical instrument;
- long-arm reaching device to get books off high shelves; and
- lightning rod, which earned him degrees from Harvard and Yale. He coined the electrical terms "positive" and "negative."

Franklin established America's first hospital in America, first postal system, a volunteer fire department, a fire insurance company, a city police force, a night watch, the lighting of city streets, a public lending library, and the University of Pennsylvania, one of America's oldest institutions of higher learning.

He studied wind speeds and water currents, their depth, speed, temperature, from the West Indies, along the Eastern coast of North America, and across the Atlantic to Europe, being the first scientist to map the Gulf Stream.

He was the first to suggest the idea of Daylight Savings Time.

In his *Poor Richard's Almanac*, May 1757, Ben Franklin wrote: "Work as if you were to live 100 years; pray as if you were to die tomorrow."

Franklin wrote May 9, 1731:

> There seems to me ... to be great occasion for raising a United Party for Virtue, by forming the virtuous and good men of all nations into a regular body ... Whoever attempts this aright, and is well qualified, cannot fail of pleasing God and of meeting with success.

At the age of 29, young Ben Franklin attended the First Presbyterian Church of Philadelphia. He wrote in his *Autobiography*:

> About the Year 1734, there arrived among us from Ireland, a young Presbyterian Preacher named Samuel Hemphill, who delivered with a good voice, and apparently extempore, most excellent discourses, which drew together considerable numbers of different persuasions, who join'd in admiring them.

> Among the rest I became one of his constant hearers, his sermons pleasing me, as they had little of the dogmatical kind, but inculcated strongly the practice of virtue, or what in the religious style are called good works ...

> Those however, of our Congregation, who considered themselves as orthodox Presbyterians, disapprov'd his doctrine, and were join'd by most of the old Clergy, who arraign'd him of heterodoxy before the Synod, in order to have him silenc'd.

> I became his zealous partisan, and contributed all I could to raise a party in his

favor; and we combated for him a while with some hopes of success. There was much scribbling pro and con upon the occasion; and finding that tho' an elegant preacher he was but a poor writer, I lent him my pen and wrote for him two or three pamphlets, and one piece in the *Pennsylvania Gazette* of April 1735.

The pamphlet titles were:

• *A Defense of the Rev. Mr. Hemphill's Observations: or, an Answer to the Vindication of the Reverend Commission* (October 30, 1735); and

• *Dialogue Between Two Presbyterians* (April 10, 1735).

These pamphlets written by Franklin contained numerous revealing statements, as recorded in *The Christian Pamphlets of Benjamin Franklin* (Fortenberry, 2014); and *Franklin on Faith: The Definitive Guide to the Religion of the First American* (Fortenberry, 2015):

• Christ gave himself for us that he might redeem us from all Iniquity, and purify to himself a peculiar people zealous of Good-Works. And there is scarcely a chapter in the whole Gospels or Epistles from which this Doctrine can't be prov'd.

• It is the duty of every Christian Minister to explode such errors which have a natural tendency to make men act as if Christ came into the world to patronize vice, and allow men to live as they please.

• I would advise these Reverend Gentlemen impartially to read the Scriptures.

• They should acknowledge Jesus Christ to be the Messiah promised by the Prophets, the Son of God.

• Those Doctrines delivered by our Savior and the Apostles, which are absolutely necessary to be believed, are so very plain, that the meanest capacities, may easily understand 'em.

• Christ by his Death and Sufferings has purchas'd for us those easy Terms and Conditions of our Acceptance with God, propos'd in the Gospel, to wit, Faith and Repentance.

• I am conscious I believe in Christ, and exert my best endeavors to understand his Will aright, and strictly to follow it.

In defense of Hemphill, Franklin wrote that:

Christianity ... is plainly nothing else, but a second Revelation of God's Will founded upon the first Revelation, which God made to us by the Light of Nature.

Despite Franklin's efforts, Rev. Samuel Hemphill was removed from preaching at the church. After this, Franklin ceased attending the church, though he continued to support it financially. He wrote in his *Autobiography*:

I had been religiously educated as a Presbyterian; and tho' some of the dogmas of that persuasion, such as the eternal decrees of God, election, reprobation, etc., appeared to me unintelligible ... I early absented myself from the public assemblies of the sect ...

I never was without some religious principles. I never doubted, for instance, the existence of the Deity; that he made the world, and govern'd it by his Providence;

that the most acceptable service of God was the doing good to man; that our souls are immortal; and that all crime will be punished, and virtue rewarded, either here or hereafter.

Franklin continued:

These I esteem'd the essentials ... found in all the religions we had in our country, I respected them all, tho' with different degrees ... This respect to all, with an opinion that the worst had some good effects, induc'd me to avoid all discourse that might tend to lessen the good opinion another might have of his own religion ...

As our province increas'd in people, and new places of worship were continually wanted, and generally erected by voluntary contributions, my mite for such purpose, whatever might be the sect, was never refused ...

Franklin added:

Tho' I seldom attended any public worship, I had still an opinion of its propriety ... and I regularly paid my annual subscription for the support of the only Presbyterian minister or meeting we had in Philadelphia.

He us'd to visit me sometimes as a friend, and admonish me to attend his administrations, and I was now and then prevail'd on to do so, once for five Sundays successively.

Had he been in my opinion a good preacher, perhaps I might have continued ... but his discourses were chiefly either polemic arguments, or explications of the peculiar doctrines of our sect, and were all to me very dry, uninteresting, and unedifying ... and I attended his preaching no more ... My conduct might be blameable, but I leave it, without attempting further to excuse it.

John Adams described Franklin:

The Catholics thought him almost a Catholic. The Church of England claimed him as one of them. The Presbyterians thought him half a Presbyterian, and the Friends believed him a wet Quaker.

When French and Spanish ships were raiding the American colonies, Ben Franklin raised Pennsylvania's first volunteer militia, beginning his public career. Franklin then proposed a General Fast, which was approved by the Colony's Council and printed in his Pennsylvania Gazette, December 12, 1747:

As the calamities of a bloody War ... seem every year more nearly to approach us ... there is just reason to fear that unless we humble ourselves before the Lord & amend our Ways, we may be chastized with yet heavier Judgments,

We have, therefore, thought fit ... to appoint ... a Day of Fasting & Prayer, exhorting all, both Ministers & People, to observe the same with becoming seriousness & attention, & to join with one accord in the most humble & fervent Supplications;

That Almighty God would mercifully interpose and still the Rage of War among the Nations & put a stop to the effusion of Christian Blood.

Franklin printed the works of Presbyterian Rev. Alexander Craighead:

- *The 1743 Renewal of the Scottish National Covenant* (1744); and
- *Solemn League and Covenant* (1748).

Rev. Craighead had anonymously written the first treatise denouncing the King of England in 1743. He left Pennsylvania for North Carolina to be the Pastor of Sugar Creek Presbyterian Church in Mecklenburg County. There, his teachings may have inspired the 1775 Mecklenburg Declaration of Independence, a precursor to Jefferson's 1776 Declaration of Independence.

Franklin published works of other prominent Great Awakening ministers: Ralph Erskine, Josiah Smith, Henry Scougal, Samuel Finley, Gilbert Tennent, Samuel Davies, and Samuel Jacob Blair.

Franklin printed the sermons of the evangelist Rev. George Whitefield, which helped to spread the Great Awakening Revival. As joint postmaster general of the colonies, he helped distribute Whitefield's sermons throughout the country.

Franklin attended Whitefield's meetings at Philadelphia's Courthouse steps, estimating 25,000 were in attendance. He described in his *Autobiography*:

> It was wonderful to see the change soon made in the manners of our inhabitants. From being thoughtless or indifferent about religion, it seemed as if all the world were growing religious, so that one could not walk thro' the town in an evening without hearing psalms sung in different families of every street.

George Whitefield wrote to Franklin in 1752:

> My Dear Doctor ... I find that you grow more and more famous in the learned world.

Franklin wrote to Whitefield:

> I sometimes wish you and I were jointly employed by the Crown to settle a colony on the Ohio ... a strong body of religious and industrious people! ... Might it not greatly facilitate the introduction of pure religion among the heathen, if we could, by such a colony, show them a better sample of Christians than they commonly see in our Indian traders?

In 1764, Franklin wrote to Whitefield, ending with the salutation:

> Your frequently repeated Wishes and Prayers for my Eternal as well as temporal Happiness are very obliging. I can only thank you for them, and offer you mine in return.

In Whitefield's last surviving letter, he shared his desire that both he and Franklin would:

> ... be in that happy number of those who is the midst of the tremendous final blaze shall cry Amen. (ref. Revelations 7:12; 19:4).

In 1749, Franklin wrote in *Proposals Relating to the Education of Youth in Pennsylvania*:

> History will also afford the frequent opportunities of showing the necessity of

a public religion, from its usefulness to the public; the advantage of a religious character among private persons ... and the excellency of the Christian religion above all others, ancient or modern.

Franklin believed Christians should be involved in meeting the needs of their communities, as he wrote to Joseph Huey, On June 6, 1753:

The worship of God is a duty; the hearing and reading of sermons may be useful; but, if men rest in hearing and praying, as too many do, it is as if a tree should value itself on being watered and putting forth leaves, though it never produce any fruit.

Franklin helped found the first hospital in America – Pennsylvania Hospital – and composed the text for the cornerstone of the hospital:

In the year of Christ, 1755 ... This building, by the bounty of the Government and of many private persons, was piously founded, for the relief of the sick and miserable. May the God of mercies bless the undertaking!

In 1754, Franklin wrote a pamphlet, "Information to Those Who Would Remove to America," for Europeans interested in sending their youth to this land:

Hence bad examples to youth are more rare in America, which must be a comfortable consideration to parents.

To this may be truly added, that serious religion, under its various denominations, is not only tolerated, but respected and practiced. Atheism is unknown there; Infidelity rare and secret; so that persons may live to a great age in that country without having their piety shocked by meeting with either an Atheist or an Infidel.

And the Divine Being seems to have manifested his approbation of the mutual forbearance and kindness with which the different sects treat each other; by the remarkable prosperity with which he has been pleased to favor the whole country.

On July 26, 1775, Franklin became the first Postmaster General of the United States, a position he held under the British Crown before the Revolution. He was a delegate to the Continental Congress where he signed the Declaration of Independence.

Franklin was chosen President (Governor) of Pennsylvania, where he signed the state's first Constitution, September 28, 1776. It was considered "the most radically democratic Frame of Government the world had ever seen." It stated in Section 10:

And each member, before he takes his seat, shall make and subscribe the following declaration, viz:

"I do believe in one God, the Creator and Governor of the Universe, the Rewarder of the good and the Punisher of the wicked. And I do acknowledge the Scriptures of the Old and New Testament to be given by Divine Inspiration. And no further or other religious test shall ever hereafter be required of any civil officer or magistrate in this State."

Pennsylvania's Constitution also stated:

Government ought to be instituted ... to enable the individuals ... to enjoy their natural rights ... which the Author of Existence has bestowed upon man; and whenever these great ends ... are not obtained, the people have a right ... to change it, and take such measures as to them may appear necessary to promote their safety and happiness ...

All men have a natural and unalienable right to worship Almighty God according to the dictates of their own consciences ... Nor can any man, who acknowledges the being of a God, be justly deprived or abridged of any civil right ... No authority ... shall in any case interfere with ... the right of conscience in the free exercise of religious worship."

Pennsylvania's Constitution had in Section 45:

Laws for the encouragement of virtue, and prevention of vice and immorality, shall be ... constantly kept in force ... Religious societies ... incorporated for the advancement of religion ... shall be encouraged.

Franklin was the first U.S. ambassador to France, where he helped negotiate and sign the Treaty of Alliance with France, 1778. He signed the Treaty of Paris, September 3, 1783, which officially ended the Revolutionary War. It began: "In the name of the Most Holy and Undivided Trinity."

As Pennsylvania's Governor, Ben Franklin hosted the Constitutional Convention in Philadelphia. During a deadlock, Franklin called for prayer, June 28, 1787:

In the beginning of the contest with Great Britain, when we were sensible of danger, we had daily prayer in this room for the divine protection. Our prayers, Sir, were heard and they were graciously answered.

All of us who were engaged in the struggle must have observed frequent instances of a superintending providence in our favor ... I therefore beg leave to move – that henceforth prayers imploring the assistance of Heaven, and its blessing on our deliberations, be held in this Assembly every morning before we proceed to business.

He was a signer of the U.S. Constitution. On April 8, 1788, Franklin wrote to the editor of the *Federal Gazette*:

I beg I may not be understood to infer, that our general Convention was divinely inspired when it form'd the new federal Constitution ...

Yet I must own I have so much faith in the general government of the world by Providence, that I can hardly conceive a transaction of such momentous importance to the welfare of millions now existing, and to exist in the posterity of a great nation, should be suffered to pass without being in some degree influenc'd, guided and governed by that omnipotent, omnipresent Beneficent Ruler, in whom all inferior spirits live and move and have their being. (Acts 17:28)

Benjamin Franklin gave advice on financial matters. In *The Way to Wealth*, 1758, he cited debt as a contributing factor to the Spanish Empire's downfall:

If you would be wealthy, says he ... think of saving as well as of getting: the Indies have not made Spain rich, because her outgoes are greater than her incomes.

Franklin expounded the dangers of debt in *The Way to Wealth*, 1758:

God gives all things to industry. Then plough deep, while sluggards sleep, and you shall have corn to sell and to keep, says Poor Dick.

Work while it is called today, for you know not how much you may be hindered tomorrow, which makes Poor Richard say, one today is worth two tomorrows; and ... have you somewhat to do tomorrow, do it today ...

And in another place, pride breakfasted with plenty, dined with poverty, and supped with infamy ... What madness must it be to run in debt for these superfluities (unnecessary expenditures) ...

We are offered, by the terms of this vendue (public auction), six months' credit; and that perhaps has induced some of us to attend it, because we cannot spare the ready money, and hope now to be fine without it ...

He continued:

When you run in debt; you give to another power over your liberty ... If you cannot pay at the time, you will be ashamed to see your creditor; you will be in fear when you speak to him, you will make poor pitiful sneaking excuses, and by degrees come to lose your veracity, and sink into base downright lying; for, as Poor Richard says, the second vice is lying, the first is running in debt ... And again to the same purpose, lying rides upon debt's back.

This is similar to the Greek historian Herodotus, who gave an account of Persia during the 5th century BC:

The most disgraceful thing in the world (as Persians) think, is to tell a lie; the next worst, to owe a debt: because, among other reasons, the debtor is obliged to tell lies.

Franklin added:

Poverty often deprives a man of all spirit ... 'tis hard for an empty bag to stand upright, as Poor Richard truly says ... And yet you are about to put yourself under that tyranny when you run in debt for such dress! Your creditor has authority at his pleasure to deprive you of your liberty, by confining you in gaol (jail) for life, or to sell you for a servant, if you should not be able to pay him!

When you have got your bargain, you may, perhaps, think little of payment; but creditors, Poor Richard tells us, have better memories than debtors ... The day comes round before you are aware, and the demand is made before you are prepared to satisfy it ...

Franklin continued:

Those have a short Lent, saith Poor Richard, who owe money to be paid at Easter. Then since, as he says, the borrower is a slave to the lender (Proverbs 22:7) and the debtor to the creditor, disdain the chain, preserve your freedom; and maintain your independency: be industrious and free; be frugal and free.

At present, perhaps, you may think yourself in thriving circumstances, and that you can bear a little extravagance without injury; but, For age and want, save while you may; No morning sun lasts a whole day, as Poor Richard says.

Gain may be temporary and uncertain, but ever while you live, expense is constant
and certain ... as Poor Richard says. So rather go to bed supperless than rise in debt.

Pennsylvania's opposition to slavery began with the Quaker Germantown Petition of 1688. Later, Anthony Benezet, a French Protestant Huguenot, joined the Quakers and convinced them at their 1758 yearly meeting in Philadelphia to officially be on record as opposing slavery. Benezet wrote in 1766, "A Caution and Warning to Great Britain ... of the Calamitous State of the Enslaved Negroes":

Slavery ... contradicted the precepts and example of Christ ... Bondage ... imposed
on the Africans, is absolutely repugnant to justice ... shocking to humanity, violative
of every generous sentiment, abhorrent utterly from the Christian religion."

In 1785, Franklin was elected president of America's first anti-slavery society, Pennsylvania Society for Promoting the Abolition of Slavery. He published several anti-slavery essays:

- *An Address to the Public* (1789);
- *A Plan for Improving the Condition of the Free Blacks* (1789); and
- *Sidi Mehemet Ibrahim on the Slave Trade* (1790).

In his last published letter (*Federal Gazette*, March 23, 1790), Franklin satirically condemned Southern state's economic argument for continuing slavery by comparing them to Muslim Barbary pirates of North Africa who enslaved Christians:

If we cease our cruises against Christians, how shall we ... make slaves of their people ... to cultivate our land ... to perform common labors ... Must we be our own slaves: And is there not more compassion due to us as Mussulmen than to these Christian dogs.

We have now about 50,000 slaves in and near Algiers ... If we then cease taking and plundering the infidel ships and making slaves of the seamen and passengers, our lands will become of no value for want of cultivation.

Less than three months before his death, Franklin signed an anti-slavery petition on February 3, 1790, and sent it to the first session of the U.S. Congress. He asked them to "devise means for removing the inconsistency from the character of the American people ... (and) promote mercy and justice toward this distressed race."

The petition was introduced in the House, February 12, 1790, and in the Senate, February 15, 1790. It stated:

For promoting the Abolition of Slavery, the relief of free Negroes unlawfully held in bondage, & the Improvement of the Condition of the African Races ... an Association was formed ... in this state by a number of her citizens of various religious denominations for promoting the abolition of Slavery ...

A just and accurate conception of the true principles of liberty ... by the blessing of Divine Providence, have been successfully directed to the relieving from bondage a large number of their fellow Creatures of the African Race ...

That mankind are all formed by the same Almighty Being, alike objects of His care and equally designed for the enjoyment of happiness the Christian Religion teaches us to believe and the political creed of America fully coincides ... that these blessings ought rightfully to be administered, without distinction of Color, to all descriptions of People ... that equal liberty ... is still the birthright of all men ...

They earnestly entreat your serious attention to the subject of Slavery ... restoration of liberty to those unhappy Men, who alone, in this land of Freedom, are degraded into perpetual Bondage ... groaning in servile subjection, that you will devise means for removing this ... promote mercy and justice towards this distressed Race, and ... for discouraging every species of traffick in the Persons of Our Fellow Men.

Philadelphia February 3, 1790

B. Franklin, President of the Society."

Southern states immediately denounced it, claiming that the Constitution limited Congress for 20 years from prohibiting the importation or emancipation of slaves.

Two months later, Franklin died on April 17, 1790, at the age of 84.

Twenty years later, President Jefferson supported the Act to end the slave trade, stating in his annual message, December 2, 1806:

I congratulate you, fellow-citizens, on the approach of the period at which you may interpose your authority constitutionally, to withdraw the citizens of the United States from all further participation in those violations of human rights which have been so long continued on the unoffending inhabitants of Africa, and which the morality, the reputation, and the best interests of our country, have long been eager to proscribe.

On March 2, 1807, Congress officially passed the Act Prohibiting the Importation of Slaves. The U.S. Navy and Coast Guard were sent to enforce the ban on importing slaves by seizing many slave trading ships. Unfortunately, slavery was not abolished until 1865 with the 13 Amendment.

Franklin had composed for his epitaph:

THE BODY of

B. FRANKLIN, Printer.

Like the cover of an old book,

Its contents torn out,

And stripped of its lettering and gilding,

Lies here, food for worms;

Yet the work itself shall not be lost,

For it will as he believ'd

appear once more,

In a new, and more beautiful edition,

Corrected and improved

By The AUTHOR.

Images of Franklin are throughout the U.S. Capitol in Washington, DC, including:

• a bust of Franklin in a window of the Library of Congress' Thomas Jefferson Building;

• in House Wing Cox Corridors, paintings of "The Constitutional Convention" and "The Declaration of Independence";

• in Senate Wing North Corridor, portrait medallion of Franklin; a lunette above a door of the Senate Committee on Foreign Relations; in Senate-side President's Room on the ceiling in a chair holding papers;

• a watercolor "Reading of the Declaration" shows Franklin on the steps with Thomas Jefferson and John Adams presenting the document to colonists.

Franklin gave a warning at the Constitutional Convention, June 28, 1787:

I have lived, Sir, a long time, and the longer I live, the more convincing proofs I see of this truth – that God governs in the affairs of men. And if a sparrow cannot fall to the ground without His notice, is it probable that an empire can rise without His aid? ...

We have been assured, Sir, in the Sacred Writings, that "except the Lord build the House, they labor in vain that build it" ... I also believe that without His concurring aid we shall succeed in this political building no better than the Builders of Babel."

Franklin wrote April 17, 1787:

Only a virtuous people are capable of freedom. As nations become corrupt and vicious, they have more need of masters.

CR

BENJAMIN BANNEKER

Benjamin Banneker (1731–1806) was a free black farmer who became a self-taught surveyor, mathematician, astronomer and author. Born near Baltimore, Maryland, his mother is thought to have been a freed indentured servant and his father a freed slave from Guinea.

In 1737, young Benjamin's name is mentioned on the deed of his family's 100-acre farm, being listed as six years old. His parents sent him to a small school where he excelled in reading, writing and arithmetic. One account stated that as a teenager, he met a Quaker named Peter Heinrich. Quakers, or the Society of Friends, was a Christian denomination known for championing equality of all races and the abolition of slavery.

Quaker Peter Heinrich founded a small school where he taught Banneker, sharing his personal library. Banneker worked the family farm and was creative in his spare time. He constructed in 1753, a large wooden clock, modeled after a pocket watch, with each piece enlarged to scale. The clock reportedly struck consistently every hour,

In 1768, Banneker put his signature on a petition to move the county seat from Joppa to Baltimore. His journals recorded observations on cicadas and the hives and behavior of honey bees

In 1772, three Quaker brothers bought land near Banneker's farm: Andrew Ellicott, John Ellicott and Joseph Ellicott. They constructed gristmills in what became Ellicott City. Banneker carefully studied all the features of how the mills worked.

Beginning in 1788, Andrew Ellicott's son, George, loaned Banneker books and equipment to study astronomy. He was soon so proficient that the next year he made astronomical calculations for planetary conjunctions and produced accurate tables for calculating solar eclipses.

He prepared an ephemeris table for 1791 and sought to have it published in an almanac. An almanac is an annual publication listing events for the upcoming year, including celestial statistics of the rising and setting times of the Sun and Moon, dates of eclipses, high and low tide tables, religious festivals, weather forecasts, and farmers' planting dates.

In 1791, U.S. Secretary of State Thomas Jefferson asked surveyor Major Andrew Ellicott to survey land that would become the District of Columbia. Ellicott hired Banneker to assist in the survey. The territory was a square, 10 miles on each side, totaling 100 square miles.

Banneker made astronomical calculations and ephemeris tables for inclusion in an almanac for the year of 1792. Andrew Elliot helped Banneker by forwarding his ephemeris tables to James Pemberton, president of the Pennsylvania Society for Promoting the Abolition of Slavery and for the Relief of Free Negroes Unlawfully Held in Bondage.

Pemberton forward Banneker's work to William Waring, a Philadelphia mathematician and ephemeris calculator, and David Rittenhouse, a prominent American astronomer who was president of the American Philosophical Society. Waring endorsed Banneker's work:

I have examined Benjamin Banneker's *Almanac* for 1792 and am of the opinion that it well deserves the acceptance and encouragement of the public.

Rittenhouse wrote that:

(Benneker's work) was a very extraordinary performance ... No doubt that the calculations are sufficiently accurate for the purposes of a common Almanac ... Every instance of genius amongst the Negroes is worthy of attention, because their suppressors seem to lay great stress on their supposed inferior mental abilities.

Banneker was pleased with Rittenhouse's endorsement, yet added:

I am annoyed to find that the subject of my race is so much stressed. The work is either correct or it is not. In this case, I believe it to be perfect.

Pemberton, with the help of Joseph Crukshank, a Quaker founder of the Pennsylvania Society for the Abolition of Slavery, arranged to have Banneker's almanac printed by William Goddard, a Baltimore printer: *Banneker's Pennsylvania, Delaware, Maryland and Virginia Almanack and Ephemeris, for the Year of our Lord, 1792.*

The *Almanac* was commercially successful with 28 editions in seven cities in five states: Baltimore; Philadelphia; Wilmington, Delaware; Alexandria, Virginia; Petersburg, Virginia; Richmond, Virginia; and Trenton, New Jersey. The title page stated:

Motions of the Sun and Moon, the True Places and Aspects of the Planets, the Rising and Setting of the Sun, Place and Age of the Moon, &c. – The Lunations, Conjunctions, Eclipses, Judgment of the Weather, Festivals, and other remarkable

Days; Days for holding the Supreme and Circuit Courts of the United States, as also the useful Courts in Pennsylvania, Delaware, Maryland, and Virginia.

Also – several useful Tables, and valuable Receipts. – Various Selections from the Commonplace–Book of the Kentucky Philosopher, an American Sage; with interesting and entertaining Essays, in Prose and Verse –the whole comprising a greater, more pleasing, and useful Variety than any Work of the Kind and Price in North America.

The *Almanac* also contained Banneker's tide table for the Chesapeake Bay region, listing the times of high tides and the methods for calculating high water at Cape Charles and Point Lookout, Virginia, Annapolis and Baltimore, Maryland, Boston, Quebec, Nantucket, Hatteras, New York, Halifax, Philadelphia and other locations.

A Philadelphia edition of *Banneker's 1795 Almanac* described a yellow fever epidemic that had struck that city in 1793, citing the origins and causes of the epidemic, as well as the extent and duration of the event.

Various editions of his almanac contained anti-slavery pleas, such as poems of abolitionist poet William Cowper, and an abolitionist essay entitled "On Negro Slavery, and the Slave Trade" which had been first published in the *Columbian Magazine*, 1790:

The time, it is hoped is not very remote, when those ill-fated people, dwelling in this land of freedom, shall commence a participation with the white inhabitants, in the blessings of liberty; and experience the kindly protection of government, for the essential rights of human nature.

Banneker's 1792 *Almanac* was presented in the British House of Commons by abolitionists William Pitt, Charles James Fox and William Wilberforce to aid their debates to end Britain's involvement in the slave trade.

Banneker included in his 1793 *Almanac* "A Plan of a Peace-Office, for the United States," authored by Dr. Benjamin Rush, a signer of the Declaration of Independence:

Let a Secretary of Peace be appointed to preside in this office ... a genuine republican and a sincere Christian ....

Let ... the Secretary ... establish ... free schools in every city, village and township in the United States .... Let the youth of our country be instructed in reading, writing, and arithmetic, and in the doctrines of a religion of some kind ... the Christian religion should be preferred to all others, for it belongs to this religion exclusively to teach us not only to cultivate peace with all men, but to forgive—nay more, to love our very enemies ....

Let every family be furnished at public expense, by the Secretary of this office, with an American edition of the Bible .... Let the following sentence be inscribed in letters of gold over the door of every home in the United States: THE SON OF MAN CAME INTO THE WORLD, NOT TO DESTROY MEN'S LIVES, BUT TO SAVE THEM."

James McHenry, a signer of the U.S. Constitution and a self-described friend of Banneker, endorsed his *Almanac* (*The American Museum,* or *Universal Magazine*):

Benjamin Banneker, a free Negro, has calculated an *Almanack*, for the ensuing year, 1792, which being desirous to dispose of, to the best advantage, he has requested me to aid his application to you for that purpose. Having fully satisfied myself, in respect to his title to this type of authorship, if you can agree to him for the price of his work, I may venture to assure you it will do you credit, as Editors, while it will afford you the opportunity to encourage talents that have thus far surmounted the most discouraging circumstances and prejudices.

In one edition, the *Almanac's* editors included a woodcut portrait of him and wrote in the preface how they:

… feel themselves gratified in the opportunity of presenting to the public, through the medium of their press, what must be considered as an extraordinary effort of genius — a complete and accurate EPHEMERIS for the Year 1792, calculated by a sable Descendant of Africa.

The introduction to a 1795 Philadelphia edition contained a poem: "Addressed to Benjamin Banneker," with verses:

Long may thou live an evidence to shew – That Afric's sable race have talents too.

And may thy genius bright its strength retain – Tho' nature to decline may still remain;

And may favour us to thy latest years – With thy Ephemeris call'd Banneker's.

In 1796, Banneker gave an *Almanac* manuscript to a member of the Ellicott family, Suzanna Mason. Suzanna's daughter published her memoirs in 1836, which included the lines:

But thou, a man exhalted high – Conspicuous in the world's keen eye …

There lived a man called Banneker – An African astronomer.

On August 30, 1791, Jefferson wrote to the Marquis de Condorcet in France, stating:

I am happy to be able to inform you that we have now in the United States a negro, the son of a black man born in Africa, and of a black woman born in the United States, who is a very respectable mathematician.

I procured him to be employed under one of our chief directors in laying out the new federal city on the Patowmac, & in the intervals of his leisure, while on that work, he made an *Almanac* for the next year, which he sent me in his own hand writing, & which I inclose to you. I have seen very elegant solutions of Geometrical problems by him. Add to this that he is a very worthy & respectable member of society.

He is a free man. I shall be delighted to see these instances of moral eminence so multiplied as to prove that the want of talents observed in them is merely the effect of their degraded condition, and not proceeding from any difference in the structure of the parts on which intellect depends.

In 1977, the Maryland Bicentennial Commission and the State Commission on Afro-American History and Culture erected a memorial obelisk near his grave near the Mount Gilboa African Methodist Episcopal Church in Oella, Maryland.

A statue of Benjamin Banneker is in the Smithsonian Institution's National Museum of African American History and Culture in Washington, D.C.

CR

REMARKABLE BLACK INNOVATORS

P AUL CUFFEE (1759–1817) was a devout Quaker Christian. His father was a freed slave from Ghana and his mother was native American of the Wampanoag tribe. Having no formal education, he learned to read and write, and studied arithmetic and navigation.

Paul Cuffee worked as a farmer, carpenter, fisherman, sea captain, sailing on whaling and cargo ships. He built a successful shipyard and shipping business, employing all black crews, sailing to the Caribbean and across the Atlantic to Europe and Africa.

During the Revolutionary War, Cuffee was arrested by the British in 1776 and spent 3 months as a captive in New York. After the war, he helped convince the Massachusetts Legislature to allow free blacks to vote in 1783.

During the War of 1812, Cuffee suffered major financial losses, but went on to found the Quaker Friendly Society of Sierra Leone, which provided money for freed slaves to build homes in Africa.

Paul Cuffee accumulated a worth over a half-million dollars, purchased a 116 acre farm in Dartmouth, Massachusetts, established the first racially integrated school in Westport, Massachusetts, and was reportedly the first African American to meet with a President, James Madison, in the White House.

JAMES FORTEN (1766–1842) grew up attending the African School run by Quaker Anthony Benezet. During the Revolution, at age 15, he joined the Continental navy, sailing with Stephen Decatur, Sr., father of the War of 1812 hero.

Forten was a crewman on the ship Royal Lewis, which was captured by the British. He was imprisoned on a British starving ship. After the war, Forten apprenticeship as a sailmaker in Philadelphia. He began his own company, invented a sail-making device and made a fortune. Employing both black and white workers, his worth was estimated at over $100,000 by the 1830s, equivalent to over $2.5 million today.

Forten helped enlist 2,500 black volunteers to defend Philadelphia during the War of 1812. He refused to do business with any vessels involved with the slave trade. Forten became a prominent advocate for abolishing of slavery, serving as vice-president of the American Anti-Slavery Society.

FREE FRANK MCWORTER (1777–1854) bought his freedom and started a saltpeter production operation – necessary for making gunpowder – which helped during the War of 1812.

His financial success enabled him to buy freedom for 16 family members, and after his death, his inheritance was used to free more. Free Frank was the first black American to found a town   New Philadelphia, Illinois, in 1836.

CLARA BROWN (1800–1885) was an ex-slave who moved to Colorado in the late 1850s during the Gold Rush. She is considered Colorado's first black settler, living in the mining town of Central City. There, she established a successful laundry business, in addition to serving as a mid-wife, cook, and nurse maid.

Clara Brown was a founding member of a Sunday school, and let her home be used for prayer services. She hosted the first Methodist church services at her house.

Affectionately called "Aunt Clara," her home was, "a hospital, a home, a general refuge for those who were sick or in poverty." She was quoted as saying, "I always go where Jesus calls me."

A Catholic Church and the first Protestant church in the Rocky Mountains were both built in part through Clara Brown's donations.

She invested in real estate and eventually owned seven houses in Central City, sixteen lots in Denver, along with interests in other properties and mines. Clara Brown was voted into the Society of Colorado Pioneers in 1885, for her role in Colorado's early history.

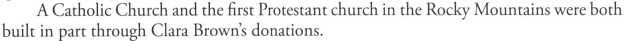

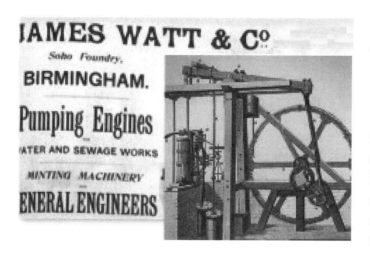

JAMES WATT & THE INDUSTRIAL REVOLUTION

At the time the colonies were being founded in America, most people were farmers or worked in trades, such as: apothecary, baker, blacksmith, butcher, cabinetmaker, carpenter, chandler (candlemaker), cobbler (shoemaker), cooper (barrelmaker), gunsmith, milliner (clothes merchant), printer, tailor, upholsterer, wheelwright (wheel craftsman).

In England, homes were heated with coal. Coal mining was an important industry and one of the dangers was mine filling up with water.

In 1712, Thomas Newcomen designed a device to pump water out of mines by using a cylinder raised by hot steam, then lowered by cool mist, on a repeating cycle, but it was inefficient. James Watt, the son of Scottish Presbyterian Covenanters, significantly improved the design by having a separate cylinder for the cool air and shut off valves.

The story is that Watt became fascinated with steam power after having observed a kettle on the stove as steam forced the lid to rise.

As recollected by Robert Hart, James Watt shared the moment of inspiration in May of 1765 for improving Thomas Newcomen's rudimentary steam engine:

> I had gone on a walk on a fine Sabbath afternoon. I had entered the Green of Glasgow by the gate at the foot of Charlotte Street— had passed the old washing-house.

> I was thinking upon the engine at the time, and had gone as far as the herd's house, when the idea came into my mind that as steam was an elastic body it would rush into a vacuum, and if a communication were made between the cylinder and an exhausted vessel it would rush into it, and might be there condensed without cooling the cylinder.

> I then saw that I must get rid of the condensed steam and injection water if I used a jet, as in Newcomen's engine. Two ways of doing this occurred to me.

> First, the water might be run off by a descending pipe, if an outlet could be got at the depth of 35 or 36 feet, and any air might be extracted by a small pump. The second was to make the pump large enough to extract both water and air ... I had not walked further than the Golf-house when the whole thing was arranged in my mind.

In 1769, Watt patented his double action steam engine with a rocking beam connected to a flywheel, which rotated in a circular arc. Speed was controlled by an ingenious invention called a centrifugal governor.

To measure the power of a steam engine, Watt introduced the measurement of "horsepower." One unit of horsepower is equal to a horse lifting 75 kilograms one meter in one second.

Watt's inventions, along with those of others, were adapted for use in: paper mills, cotton textile manufacturing, locomotives, and steamboats. This was called the Industrial Revolution.

In honor of James Watt, German-British engineer C. William Siemens proposed in 1882 naming a unit of power a "watt."

Steam was soon harnessed to not just power pumps, but textile manufacturing machines. This led to the creation of factories which could mass produce items inexpensively. European manufactured products were imported into America, which was soon followed Americans building factories.

ROBERT FULTON
& THE STEAMBOAT

Inventors began to explore using steam to power railroad engines and steamboats. Ben Franklin had written on using steam to propel boats and supported the earlier inventor James Rumsey in his attempt develop steam-powered jet propulsion.

In 1787, American John Fitch adapted a steam engine to power a boat – a steamboat. Fitch had a patented design to use a steam engine attached to a bank of oars to paddle the boat. His model proved to too expensive for practical use. Ronald Reagan commented, May 20, 1986:

> When steam-powered vessels began to eclipse sailing ships in the latter part of the 19th century, it was largely the result of pioneering work by two Americans, John Fitch and Robert Fulton.

As a young man, Robert Fulton had met Benjamin Franklin. Fulton went to France where he successfully developed the first practical submarine in 1800, but Napoleon was uninterested.

When told of Robert Fulton's plan for a steam-powered engine, Napoleon replied:

ROBERT FULTON'S STEAMBOAT "CLERMONT"

What, sir? You would make a ship sail against the wind and currents by lighting a bonfire under her decks? I pray you excuse me. I have no time to listen to such nonsense.

Robert Fulton secured the financial backing of New York founding father Chancellor Robert Livingston, who was on the committee with Jefferson to draft the Declaration of Independence.

With Livingston's support, Robert Fulton built in 1806 the first commercial steamboat, *Clermont*, with a circular wooden paddle wheel. In 1807, the *Clermont* carried passengers 150 miles from New York City to the state capital of Albany in just 32 hours.

In *The Thorny Road of Honor*, 1856, Hans Christian Anderson wrote:

We are in America, on the margin of one of the largest rivers, an innumerable crowd has gathered, for it is said that a ship is to sail against the wind and weather ... The man who thinks he can solve the problem is named Robert Fulton ...

The ship begins its passage, but suddenly stops. The crowd begins to laugh ... Then suddenly ... the wheels turn again ... the ship continues its course ... between the builder of the bridge and the earth – between Providence and the human race.

Called "the father of steam navigation," Robert Fulton wrote about his first trip from

New York City to Albany on the ship *Clermont*, August 7, 1807:

> The power of propelling boats by steam is now fully proved. The morning I left New York there were not perhaps thirty persons in the city who believed that the boat would ever move one mile an hour or be of the least utility; and, while we were putting off from the wharf, which was crowded with spectators, I heard a number of sarcastic remarks ...

Fulton continued:

> It was the early autumn of the year 1807 that a knot of villagers was gathered on a high bluff just opposite Poughkeepsie, on the west bank of the Hudson, attracted by the appearance of a strange, dark looking craft, which was slowly making its way up the river. Some imagined it to be a sea monster, while others did not hesitate to express their belief that it was a sign of the approaching judgment.

> What seemed strange in the vessel was the ... lofty and straight black smoke-pipes rising from the deck, instead of the gracefully tapered masts ... The working-beam and pistons and the slow turning and splashing of the huge and naked paddle-wheels met the astonished gaze. The dense clouds of smoke, as they rose wave upon wave, added still more to the wonderment of the rustics.

Robert Fulton's statue was placed in the U.S. Capitol's Statuary Hall by the State of Pennsylvania in 1889. Ronald Reagan stated June 11, 1981:

> The future has always looked bleak til people with brains and faith ... found a

way to make it better, people like Robert Fulton.

An honorable mention is given to Samuel Morey, who successfully invented a steam power paddle wheel, but he lacked financial backing, and John Stevens built a type of screw-driven steamboat in 1802.

The *SS Savannah* left May 22, 1819, from Savannah, Georgia, and 25 days later arrived in Liverpool, England, completing the first trans-Atlantic voyage by steamship.

Ninety percent of the world's goods are transported by sea and the waterways. There are approximately 1.2 million seafarers worldwide in 10,000 commercial ships and maritime vessels. To pay tribute to the American Merchant Marine, President Franklin Roosevelt designated MAY 22, 1933, as NATIONAL MARITIME DAY.

On National Maritime Day in Washington, D.C., 2012, Rev. Canon James D. Von Dreele, Vice President of the North American Maritime Ministry Association, stated:

> Not a ship in ancient times was launched or set out on a voyage without proper prayers ... The Bible is filled with sailing images and some of Jesus' disciples were fishermen. Seafarers ... look for special blessings for their ships from the church ...
>
> The launching of new builds requires a minister to bless the ship ... Maritime ministry got its start in America in the early 1800's. Earnest church clergy and laity formed missions in Boston, New York and Philadelphia, the prime ports of this nascent nation ... Their prime concerns were the religious, moral and physical well-being of seafarers.

CR

NOTEWORTHY BLACK MERCHANTS

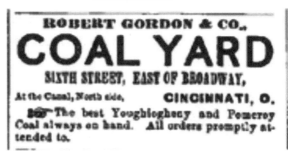

Williams 1859

ROBERT GORDON & CO.,
COAL YARD
SIXTH STREET, EAST OF BROADWAY,
At the Canal, North side, CINCINNATI, O.
The best Youghiogheny and Pomeroy Coal always on hand. All orders promptly attended to.

R OBERT GORDON (1812–1884) was a slave who worked in a coal yard in Richmond, Virginia. He was so diligent that the owner gave him control of the enterprise, selling to manufacturers and blacksmiths.

His owner allowed him to have the "slack" – coal dust that covered the yard, which Gordon made useful to industrial customers. Within a few years, Gordon was able to buy his freedom in 1846.

In 1847, he traveled to Ohio, a free state, and invested $15,000 in land in Cincinnati on the Miami Canal at Eighth and Lock Streets. He hired bookkeepers and bought and sold coal by the boatload. Soon, other coal yards tried to put him out of business with a "coal war," drastically reducing their prices to undercut his sales. In a shrewd business decision, rather than lower his prices, Gordon employed mulattoes, mixed-race men who could pass as whites, to buy up his competitor's cheaper coal and stockpile it.

When waterways along the Ohio River froze, preventing his competition from acquiring more coal, Gordon's large coal reserves allowed his business to expand, bringing respect from the business community.

The weekly newspaper, *Catholic Telegraph*, began carrying his advertisement in 1849 "Robert Gordon & Co. Coal Yard, Sixth St., east of Broadway, near the Canal."

In September of 1849, Gordon married free born Eliza Jane Cressup, the daughter of a black carpenter named Thomas Crissup. Their neighborhood was the location of Allen Temple African Methodist Episcopal Church, founded in 1824. It was the first worship space of its kind west of the Alleghenies. The church formed the Freedmen's Aid Society, with Mrs. Eliza Gordon as President.

When the Civil War began, Gordon donated 25 bushels of coal to Cincinnati's Military Hospital, May 1861. In 1865, Gordon retired and invested his money in U.S. bonds and in real estate in Walnut Hills, Cincinnati. By the time of his death in 1884, Robert Gordon's estate was worth $200,000, equivalent to $5 million today.

Considered the wealthiest black man in the State of Ohio, he left in his Will, as reported in the Chicago Conservator:

$25,000 for the establishment of a home for aged and indigent colored women in Cincinnati. A bequest of $1,000 is made to the colored orphan asylum.

S TEPHEN SMITH (1795–1873), was an indentured servant in Pennsylvania, assigned to work in the lumberyards by his master Thomas Boude. At the age of 21, he borrowed $50 and purchased his freedom, after which he soon married Harriet Lee.

Smith continued work in lumberyards, saving his money, till he could open his own lumber business in 1822. His business grew from lumber to real estate and coal. His success was met with being vandalized and burned, but he restarted it.

Stephen Smith became one of the wealthiest businessmen in Pennsylvania and served on the board of a bank. By the 1850s, he was grossing $100,000 in annual sales and by 1857, he worth was approximately $500,000 (equivalent to $13.5 million today).

Smith was involved in religious activities as a minister and served as chairman of the black abolitionist organization in Columbia, Pennsylvania.

WILLIAM ALEXANDER LEIDESDORFF, JR. (1810–1848) was of African, Cuban, and Jewish descent. He arrived in San Francisco in 1841 and proceeded to establish a shipyard, a lumber yard, and a ship chandlery shop, which supplied equipment for steamboats and sailing ships.

As one of the richest residents in San Francisco, William Alexander Leidesdorff built the city's first hotel and first public school.

He was the city treasurer and was proponent of California becoming a U.S. State. Considered America's first black millionaire, Leidesdorff's worth in 1856 was valued at $1.4 million, equivalent to over $20 million today.

CR

JOHN ERICSSON & THE IRONCLAD MONITOR

In 1836, John Ericsson invented a hot air pump and a patented a screw propeller, which significantly improved steamship propulsion and was less vulnerable in battle as compared to paddle wheels.

In 1839, the U.S. Navy Captain Robert Stockton invited Ericsson to come to America to design the sloop *USS Princeton*, with new steam driven twin screw propellers and smokestacks. Launched in 1843, the *USS Princeton* won speed trials over steam paddle boats, making it the fastest steamer afloat.

Unfortunately, during a demonstration in 1844, a faulty cannon exploded, killing the Secretary of the Navy and the Secretary of State. Fortunately for him, President John Tyler was safe below deck.

In 1845, nine years after the Battle of the Alamo, Robert Stockton sailed the *USS Princeton* to Galveston with President James Polk's offer to annex Texas. Fort Stockton, Texas, is named for him.

Stockton is most remembered for sailing a fleet in 1846 to California, on by his flagship *USS Congress*. He captured the state and sent word by land back to Washington, D.C., carried by Kit Carson. Stockton, California, is named after him.

John Ericsson continued making naval innovations:
• a boilerless hot air caloric engine,
• the first submarine boat,
• the first self-propelled torpedo, and
• the first torpedo boat.

Ericcson presented a design for an iron-clad armored battleship to France's Napoleon III in 1854, but he did not pursue it.

Using a steam-powered screw propeller, the frigate *USS Merrimack* was launched in 1855 in Boston Navy Yard. It also had masts and sails to conserve on coal which was needed to burn and make steam. It named after the Merrimack River that flows through New Hampshire and Massachusetts.

The *USS Merrimack* sailed to: Southampton, England; Brest in northwestern France; Lisbon, Portugal; and Toulon, and southern France. In 1857, it sailed around Cape Horn, South America, and cruised the Pacific coast of South and Central America. In 1860, *USS Merrimack* was decommissioned for repairs in Norfolk, Virginia.

When the Civil War started, a Union naval office tried to get the *USS Merrimack* out of the Norfolk harbor, but sunken ships blocked the way. To prevent capture, it was partially burned and sunk.

The Confederate Navy, desperate for ships, salvaged the *USS Merrimack* from the water and repaired it, transforming it into an "ironclad," with its hull and deck covered with iron plates, and 14 gun ports with iron shutters. The Confederate navy renamed it the *CSS Virginia*, though many still referred to it as *Merrimack*.

The Union Navy was blockading the James River as it entered Chesapeake Bay, thus cutting off Virginia's largest cities, Richmond and Norfolk, from international trade.

On the morning of March 8, 1862, the Battle of Hampton Roads began. The Confederate iron-plated *CSS Virginia* (*Merrimack*) attacked, destroying numerous vessels, including two Union boats, *USS Congress* and *USS Cumberland*, and running a third aground in shallow water, the *USS Minnesota*.

The next day, the *CSS Virginia* (*Merrimack*) sailed out to continue its attacks but during the night, the Union the ironclad, *USS Monitor*, had sailed into the waters of Hampton Roads. The *USS Monitor* was designed by John Ericsson, who had presented plans for it to the U.S. Navy in 1861 based on the dimensions of a Swedish lumber raft. It had a revolving gun turret designed by American inventor Theodore Timby.

President Calvin Coolidge dedicated a memorial to John Ericsson, May 29, 1926:

> The Confederate ironclad ... *Merrimack* began a work of destruction among 16 Federal vessels, carrying 298 guns .... When the ironclad *Merrimack* went out on the morning of March 9 to complete its work of destruction it was at once surprised and challenged by this new and extraordinary naval innovation ...
>
> After a battle lasting four hours in which the *Monitor* suffered no material damage

... the *Merrimack* ... badly crippled, withdrew, never to venture out again ...

The London Times stated that the day before this battle England had 149 first-class warships. The day after she had but two, and they were iron-plated only amidships. Naval warfare had been revolutionized.

Coolidge continued his dedication speech to 5,000 people assembled at the John Ericsson Memorial, one block south of the Lincoln Memorial, May 29, 1926:

> We assemble here today to do reverence to the memory of a great son of Sweden ... John Ericsson ... We honor him most of all because we can truly say he was a great American.

With Sweden's Crown Prince Gustav Adolf in attendance at the dedication, President Coolidge described Ericsson's home country:

> Sweden is a country where existence has not been easy. Lying up under the Arctic Circle ... At an early period they were converted to the Christian faith and their natural independence made them early responsive to the Protestant Reformation, in which their most famous king, Gustavus Adolphus, "The Lion of the North," was one of the most militant figures in the movement for a greater religious freedom ...

It was under this great leader that plans were first matured to establish a colony in this country for purpose of trade and in order that the native, as was set out in the charter, might be "made more civilized and taught morality and the Christian religion ... besides the further propagation of the Holy Gospel" ...

While it was under a new charter that a Swedish colony finally reached the Delaware in 1638, they never lost sight of their original purpose, but among other requests kept calling on the mother country for ministers, Bibles, and Psalm books ...

Coolidge described the Swedes further:

Forty-one clergymen came to America prior to 1779. One of the historians of this early settlement asserts that these colonists laid the basis for a religious structure, built the first flour mills, the first ships, the first brickyards, and made the first roads, while they introduced horticulture and scientific forestry into this Delaware region ...

The building of nearly 2,000 churches and nearly as many schools stands to their credit ... Always as soon as they have provided shelter for themselves they have turned to build places of religious worship and founded institutions of higher learning with the original purpose of training clergymen and teachers ... Reverence for religion ... is the foundation of moral power.

Calvin Coolidge spoke further on the subject of Swedes:

Though few in number during the period of our Revolutionary War, they supported the Colonial cause and it has been said that King Gustavus III, writing to a friend, declared "If I were not King I would proceed to America and offer my sword of behalf of the brave Colonies" ... Such is the background and greatness of the Swedish people in the country of their origin and in America that gave to the world John Ericsson.

When offered payment for designing the *USS Monitor*, John Ericsson, who "had a particular horror of slavery," replied to a U.S. Senator in 1882:

> Nothing could induce me to accept any remuneration from the United States for the Monitor ... It was my contribution to the glorious Union cause ... which freed 4,000,000 bondsmen.

In Battery Park, New York City, a bronze portrait of John Ericsson was dedicated in 1893, and a statue in 1903, with the plaque:

> The City of New York erects this statue to the memory of a citizen whose genius has contributed to the greatness of the Republic and the progress of the world ... JOHN ERICSSON was born in Langsbanshyttan, Sweden, July 31, 1803, died in New York, March 8, 1889.

Considered one of the greatest mechanical engineers in history, a monument was dedicated to him in Nybroviken, Stockholm. The United States issued a postage stamp honoring John Ericsson in 1926. A memorial erected to John Ericsson and the *Monitor* in McGolrick Park, Brooklyn, NY, in 1939:

> Erected by the people of the State of New York to commemorate the Battle of the

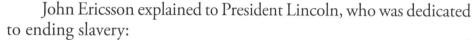

Monitor and *Merrimack*, March 9, 1862, and in memory of the men of the *Monitor* and its designer John Ericsson.

President Coolidge concluded his tribute to John Ericsson:

This great mechanical genius wrote to President Lincoln offering to "construct a vessel for the destruction of the hostile fleet in Norfolk and for scouring southern rivers and inlets of all craft protected by southern batteries."

John Ericsson explained to President Lincoln, who was dedicated to ending slavery:

Attachment to the Union alone impels me to offer my services at this frightful crisis – my life if need be – in the great cause which Providence has caused you to defend.

Ericsson stated:

I love this country. I love its people and its laws, and I would give my life for it."

☙

SAMUEL F.B. MORSE & THE TELEGRAPH

The world of communication was revolutionized by a man who died April 2, 1872. His name was Samuel F.B. Morse, inventor of the Telegraph and the Morse Code.

Samuel F.B. Morse graduated from Yale in 1810 and became one of the greatest portrait artists. He founded the National Academy of Design and served as its president for 20 years.

In 1831, Morse was appointed to the first chair of fine arts in America, the Professor of Sculpture and Painting at New York University.

Morse obtained a patent for his telegraph but found it difficult to get financial backers. During the anxious days between failure and success, Samuel F.B. Morse wrote to his wife:

> The only gleam of hope, and I cannot underrate it, is from confidence in God. When I look upward it calms my apprehensions for the future, and I seem to hear a voice saying: "If I clothe the lilies of the field, shall I not also clothe you?" Here is my strong confidence, and I will wait patiently for the direction of Providence.

In 1843, Congress agreed to underwrite Morse to erect the first telegraph lines between Baltimore and the U.S. Supreme Court chamber in Washington, D.C.

Samuel F.B. Morse demonstrated the telegraph for the first time on May 24, 1844, allowing Annie Ellsworth, the young daughter of a friend, to choose the message. She selected a verse from the Bible, Numbers 23:23, "What hath God wrought?"

The Morse Code, considered the first digital binary code, became an international means of telecommunications. It revolutionized the transfer of information and knowledge worldwide, becoming the basis for all later advancements in communication.

Four years before his death, Samuel F.B. Morse wrote:

> The nearer I approach to the end of my pilgrimage, the clearer is the evidence of the divine origin of the Bible, the grandeur and sublimity of God's remedy for fallen man are more appreciated, and the future is illumined with hope and joy.

Samuel F.B. Morse was the son of educator Jedediah Morse, known as "Father of American Geography." Jedediah Morse published:

- *Geography Made Easy*, 1784,
- *The American Geography*, 1789;
- *Elements of Geography*, 1795;
- *The American Gazetteer*, 1797;
- *A New Gazetteer of the Eastern Continent*, 1802;
- *A Compendious History of New England*, 1804; and
- *Annals of the American Revolution*.

Jedediah Morse founded the New England Tract Society in 1814, and the American Bible Society in 1816. He was a member of the American Board of Commissioners for

Foreign Missions, 1811–19.

In an "Election Sermon" given at Charleston, Massachusetts, April 25, 1799, Jedediah Morse stated:

> To the kindly influence of Christianity we owe that degree of civil freedom, and political and social happiness which mankind now enjoys. In proportion as the genuine effects of Christianity are diminished in any nation, either through unbelief, or the corruption of its doctrines, or the neglect of its institutions; in the same proportion will the people of that nation recede from the blessings of genuine freedom, and approximate the miseries of complete despotism. I hold this to be a truth confirmed by experience ...

Jedediah Morse concluded:

> If so, it follows, that all efforts to destroy the foundations of our holy religion, ultimately tend to the subversion also of our political freedom and happiness. Whenever the pillars of Christianity shall be overthrown, our present republican forms of government, and all the blessings which flow from them, must fall with them.

On his tombstone is written:

> In memory of Jedediah Morse – The Father of American Geography – Born in Woodstock, Windham Co. Conn. – Aug. 23, 1761 – Died in New Haven, June 9, 1826 – In the Joy of a Triumphant Faith in Christ.

❧

EARLY BLACK ENTREPRENEURS

ANTOINE DUBUCLET (1810–1887) was born in 1810 Louisiana to free black parents. He inherited his father's sugar plantation of over 400 acres. He married Claire Pollard, a successful free black woman, and their combined assets were estimated at over $95,000, making them some of the wealthiest planters of their day. They had 9 children, whom they sent to France for education, with several daughters marrying Frenchmen and remaining there. Two sons earned medical degrees.

The Civil War devastated the state's sugar industry, but Dubuclet recovered and in 1868 was elected as a Republican to be Louisiana State Treasurer, the first African American to hold that office. Taking charge of the bankrupt state's finances, Dubuclet, with others in the administration, successfully reduced the state's enormous debt and restored solvency.

Being lauded by both Democrats and Republicans, he was reelected in 1870 and again in 1874. Dubuclet was the only officeholder to remain in office after a coup attempt known as the Battle of Liberty Place, September 1874. He also survived an impeachment attempt in 1876. Dying in 1887, Antoine Dubuclet was buried New Orlean's St. Louis Cemetery No. 2 and inducted into the Louisiana Black History Hall of Fame in 1990.

M ARY ELLEN PLEASANT (1814–1904) was born a slave but worked out her bondage. She was joined with white abolitionists in Massachusetts to help slaves get to freedom through the Underground Railroad.

In 1852, Mary arrived in San Francisco where she founded exclusive men's eating establishments. Paying attention to business tips, she invested and eventually amassed millions of dollars.

Mary Ellen Pleasant's work with the Underground Railroad continued, resulting in her being considered the "Harriett Tubman of California."

R OBERT JAMES HARLAN (1816–1897) was a light-skinned black slave from Kentucky whose master, and possible father, allowed him to pursue training and trading horses. He moved to California in 1849, where he made a fortune running a store in early in days of the Gold Rush.

He moved to England in 1859, where he raced American horses. In 1869, Robert Harlan returned to the United States during the "Reconstruction Era."

He became friends with Ulysses S. Grant and got involved in Republican politics as a champion for African American civil rights. Harlan served as colonel of Cincinnati's black state militia – the Second Ohio Militia Battalion – and in 1886 was elected to the Ohio House of Representatives.

ෆ

DR. IGNAZ PHILIPP SEMMELWEIS & HAND WASHING

Washing hands to prevent the spread of disease was recommended in 1844 to the doctors of the Vienna General Hospital by Dr. Ignaz Philipp Semmelweis.

He noticed that doctors would go straight from doing autopsies on those who died of puerperal fever to delivering babies and soon after the mothers would die of puerperal fever.

Nearly 25 percent of all mothers giving birth in hospital maternity wards died of puerperal fever, with epidemics sometimes reaching 100 percent.

Dr. Ignaz Semmelweis was ridiculed so much for his "handwashing" suggestion that he was forced to leave Vienna and eventually died in a mental asylum.

℞

DR. OLIVER WENDELL HOLMES, SR.

In America, Dr. Oliver Wendell Holmes, Sr., made the same suggestion, publishing an article "The Contagiousness of Puerperal Fever" (*New England Quarterly Journal of Medicine and Surgery*, 1843).

Holmes, who coined the word "anesthesia," recommended that after doctors examined patients that died of fatal illness, they should purify their instruments and burn contaminated clothing, stating:

> I beg to be heard in behalf of the women whose lives are at stake, until some stronger voice shall plead for them.

Holmes was born in Cambridge, Massachusetts, August 29, 1809, just north of Harvard Yard in the house where patriots planned the Battle of Bunker Hill. His father was Abiel Holmes, minister of the First Congregational Church in Cambridge.

Dr. Oliver Wendell Holmes, Sr., was dean of Harvard Medical School, where he taught Anatomy, Pathology, and Physiology for 35 years. He introduced the use of the microscope in medical education.

Before the discovery of "germs," Holmes was ridiculed by academia for promoting the novel practice of doctors washing their hands and surgical instruments to prevent the spread of diseases, a conclusion which Dr. Ignaz Semmelweis also reached in Vienna, Austria.

Dr. Holmes caused a controversy by trying to admit the first woman and the first African-Americans to Harvard Medical School.

He invented the "American stereoscope," which was a 19th century hand held device to view 3-D pictures.

Oliver Wendell Holmes, Sr., was one of the popular America's Fireside Poets. He wrote:

- Some people are so heavenly minded that they are no earthly good.

- Most people are willing to take the Sermon on the Mount as a flag to sail under, but few will use it as a rudder by which to steer.

- I find the great thing in this world is not so much where we stand, as in what direction we are moving: To reach the port of Heaven, we much sail sometimes with the wind and sometimes against it – but we must sail, and not drift, nor lie at anchor.

Dr. Holmes' son, Oliver Wendell Holmes, Jr., was appointed to the Supreme Court by Theodore Roosevelt in 1902.

Just as with Dr. Ignaz Semmelweis, medical professionals criticized Holmes for his hand washing recommendations, and as a result, a high number of soldiers died during the Civil War from infections. When Louis Pasteur confirmed the existence of microscopic germs, "handwashing" became accepted in medical practice as a way to prevent the spread of disease.

CR

LOUIS PASTEUR

Louis Pasteur became a professor of chemistry at the University of Strasbourg, where in 1849 he married Marie Laurent, daughter of the University's rector.

Tragically, three of their five children died of typhoid, which led him to research the causes and prevention of diseases.

Louis Pasteur's study of micro-organisms and his germ theory revolutionized medicine. He developed vaccines for rabies and anthrax, drawing on Edward Jenner's 1796 method of inoculating people from smallpox by "vaccinating" them with cowpox – ("vaca" being Latin for cow).

Louis Pasteur laid the foundation for the control of tuberculosis, cholera, diphtheria and tetanus – diseases which had killed millions. He, along with Ferdinand Cohn and Robert Koch, are considered the fathers of the science of microbiology.

Louis Pasteur described anaerobic (without oxygen) bacteria:

> The more I study nature, the more I stand amazed at the work of the Creator.
> Into his tiniest creatures, God has placed extraordinary properties that turn them into agents of destruction of dead matter.

In *The Life of Louis Pasteur*, written by Rene' Vallery-Radot, translated by Mrs. R.L. Devonshire, (McClure, Phillips & Co., 1902, Vol. 1, p. 260–262), Pasteur wrote in a notebook, 1871:

Life is in the germ, that it has been but in a state of transmission since the origin of creation.

In an interview with the Mayor and the President of the Chamber of Commerce of Orleans, France, Louis Pasteur talked of:

Science, which brings man nearer to God.

Louis Pasteur, as Dean of the Faculty of Sciences at Lille University in France. He researched how micro-organisms spoiled beverages, such as beer, wine and milk.

In January of 1860, he wrote to Chappuis (Vallery-Radot, *Life of Louis Pasteur*):

I am pursuing as best I can these studies on fermentation which are of great interest, connected as they are with the impenetrable mystery of Life and Death.

Pasteur developed the process of heating the liquids to kill most bacteria and molds, which became called "pasteurization." President Eisenhower wrote January 8, 1954:

Pasteurization of milk has prevented Countless epidemics and saved thousands of lives.

As a young man, Louis Pasteur wrote to his sisters, November 1, 1840 (Rene' Vallery-Radot, *The Life of Louis Pasteur*, Vol. I, NY: McClure, Phillips & Co., 1902):

These three things, WILL, WORK, SUCCESS, fill human existence. WILL opens the door to success both brilliant and happy; WORK passes these doors;

and at the end of the journey SUCCESS comes to crown one's efforts. And so, my dear sisters, if your resolution is firm, your task ... is already begun; You have but to walk forward ...

If perchance you should falter during the journey, a hand would be there to support you. If that should be wanting, God, who alone could take that hand from you, would Himself accomplish its work.

At his formal inauguration to the Faculty of Letters of Douai and the Faculty of Sciences of Lille, Louis Pasteur remarked, December 7, 1854:

Dans les champs de l'observation, le hasard ne favorise que les esprits préparés (In the field of observation, chance favors only the prepared mind.)

President George H.W. Bush referred to this statement, February 13, 1989:

You know, Louis Pasteur once said: "Chance favors only the prepared mind" ... For America to be prepared for the future, our children must be educated.

Pasteur wrote to his father, February 7, 1860 (Vallery-Radot, *Life of Louis Pasteur*):

God grant that by my persevering labors I may bring a little stone to the frail and ill-assured edifice of our knowledge of those deep mysteries of Life and Death where all our intellects have so lamentably failed.

Pasteur stated (Albert Keim & Louis Lumet, *Louis Pasteur*, NY, 1914: trans. F.T. Cooper, Frederick A. Stokes Co, p. 143):

Are science, and the passionate desire to understand, anything else than the effect of that spur towards knowledge which the mystery of the universe has placed in our souls? Where are the true sources of human dignity, of liberty, of modern democracy, unless they are contained in the idea of the infinite, before which all men are equal?

Upon his father's death, Pasteur wrote (Vallery-Radot, *Life of Louis Pasteur*):

> Dear children, the dear grandfather is no more ... Until the last moment I hoped I should see him again, embrace him for the last time ... He died on the day of your first communion, dear Cécile; those two memories will remain in your heart ... I was asking you to pray for the grandfather at Arbois College. Your prayers will have been acceptable unto God, and perhaps the dear grandfather himself knew of them and rejoiced with dear little Jeanne over Cécile's piety.

In *The Life of Louis Pasteur*, written by Rene' Vallery-Radot, translated by Mrs. R.L. Devonshire, (Vol. I, NY: McClure, Phillips & Co., 1902, p. 257), Pasteur wrote:

> Great discoveries ... introduce into the whole of Society that philosophical or scientific spirit, that spirit of discernment, which submits everything to severe reasoning, condemns ignorance and scatters errors and prejudices. They raise the intellectual level and the moral sense, and through them the Divine idea itself is spread abroad and intensified.

In the book, *Louis Pasteur* by Patrice Debre', translated by Eblorg Forster (John Hopkins University Press, 1998), Louis Pasteur is quoted as saying:

> In each one of us there are two men, the scientist and the man of faith or of

doubt. These two spheres are separate, and woe to those who want to make them encroach upon one another in the present state of our knowledge!

President Lyndon B. Johnson stated April 7, 1966:

> Years ago Louis Pasteur said, "I hold the unconquerable belief that science and peace will triumph over ignorance and war; that nations will come together not to destroy, but to construct; and that the future belongs to those who accomplish most for humanity."

In 1888, the Pasteur Institute was founded in France. Louis Pasteur stated in his inaugural speech (Vallery-Radot 1901, 2, p. 289):

> Two opposing laws seem to me now to be in contest. The one seeks violent conquests, the other, the relief of mankind. The one places a single life above all victories, the other sacrifices hundreds of thousands of lives to the ambition of a single individual.
>
> The law of which we are the instruments strives even through the carnage to cure the wounds due to the law of war. Treatment by our antiseptic methods may preserve the lives of thousands of soldiers. Which of these two laws will prevail, God only knows. But of this we may be sure, science, in obeying the law of humanity, will always labor to enlarge the frontiers of life.

A Catholic, though sometimes described as a free thinker, Louis Pasteur died on September 28, 1895, while listening to the story of the French priest St. Vincent de Paul,

who had been enslaved by Muslim Barbary pirates in Tunis, North Africa, 1605, and escaped two years later

In 1605, St. Vincent de Paul was sailing from Marseille, France, when he was captured by Muslim Barbary pirates. He was auctioned off into slavery in Tunis, North Africa. Fortunately, after two years, St. Vincent de Paul was able to convert his owner to Christianity in 1607. He escaped to Europe where he started religious orders to care for the poor and suffering in hospitals.

Shortly after his death, Pasteur was attributed with the quotation:

The more I know, the more does my faith approach that of the Breton peasant. Could I but know all, I would have the faith of a Breton peasant woman.

As recorded in *The Life of Louis Pasteur* (Rene' Vallery-Radot, 1911, vol. 2, p. 240), Pasteur's son-in-law gave this description of him:

Absolute faith in God and in Eternity, and a conviction that the power for good given to us in this world will be continued beyond it, were feelings which pervaded his whole life; the virtues of the gospel had ever been present to him. Full of respect for the form of religion which had been that of his forefathers, he came simply to it and naturally for spiritual help in these last weeks of his life.

Being one of the first European scientists to reject the evolutionary theory of spontaneous generation, Louis Pasteur insisted that life only arises from life, stating:

> Microscopic beings must come into the world from parents similar to themselves ... There is something in the depths of our souls which tells us that the world may be more than a mere combination of events.

෪

DR. JOSEPH LISTER

Louis Pasteur's studies of infectious microbiology influenced Dr. Joseph Lister in Scotland to pioneer sterile surgery. "Listerine" antiseptic mouthwash was named for him. He stated: "I am a believer in the fundamental doctrines of Christianity."

Dr. Joseph Lister told a graduating class:

> It is our proud office to tend the fleshly tabernacle of the immortal spirit, and our path, if rightly followed, will be guided by unfettered truth and love unfeigned. In pursuit of this noble and holy calling I wish you all God-speed.

෪

BLACK BUSINESS PIONEERS

Bridget "Biddy" Mason (1818–1901) was a slave who had three daughters by her slave master Robert Smith. Smith converted to Mormonism and moved to Utah, forcing Bridget to follow the wagon on foot.

In 1851, Smith moved again, this time to California. Though it was a free state, Smith refused to abide by the laws and he kept Biddy a slave. When Smith decided to move to Texas, a slave state, a white man, Charles Owens, helped bring legal action to gain Biddy's freedom.

After a fierce court battle, Biddy Mason won in 1856. Charles Owens soon married Biddy's daughter Ellen. Biddy worked as a mid-wife, delivering hundreds of babies. When a smallpox epidemic hit, she risked her life to care for multitudes who were infected.

Saving her money, she purchased two estates, making her one of the first black women to own property in Los Angeles. She bought more properties and leased them out commercially. As the city grew, her properties appreciated in value, resulting in her amassing a relatively large fortune of $300,000.

In 1872, along with her son-in-law Charles Owens, she organized the city's first black church, the First African Methodist Episcopal Church of Los Angeles, which met in her home on Spring Street.

Being the wealthiest black woman in the city, Biddy Mason donated the land and helped finance the building of the church. She also established the first elementary school for black children in Los Angeles.

SAMUEL T. WILCOX went from a boat steward on the Ohio River to building a high-quality wholesale and retail grocery business in Cincinnati in the 1850s. He also founded a pickling and preserving business.

Wilcox had commercial links and markets in New York, New Orleans, Boston and Baltimore.

He only sold premium-quality goods, such as hams, dried fruit, sugar, and soaps, which attracted the most affluent customers. He started business with $25,000 and made nearly $140,000 in annual sales, which equates to around $4.2 million in today's money.

I SAAC MYERS (1835–1891) was an influential figure in creating one of the first African American trade unions. He began this effort after the Civil War when 1,000 black ship caulkers lost employment in Baltimore.

Myers organized them into the Colored Caulkers Trade Union Society. As other black workers faced opposition, he helped establish the Colored National Labor Union. Following his term as its president, he was succeeded by Frederick Douglass.

J OHN MERRICK (1859–1919), AARON MCDUFFIE MOORE (1863–1923) and CHARLES CLINTON SPAULDING (1874–1952) founded the North Carolina Mutual Life Insurance Company in 1898 – the now-oldest and largest African-American life insurance company in the United States. The company still exists, with assets of $162 million.

At the time of the company's founding in 1898, Durham, North Carolina, was referred to as "Black Wall Street" for the economic successes blacks were having in business.

M AGGIE LENA WALKER (1864–1934) was the first black woman in the United States to charter a bank. By pooling her community's money, she formed the St. Luke Penny Savings Bank, of which she served as the first president.

Later, when the bank merged with two other Richmond, VA banks to form The Consolidated Bank and Trust Company, she served as the chairman of its board of directors. She stated:

- Friends and good manners will take you where money won't go.

- If you can read and write, you can do anything and go anywhere. You can ride the wind.

F REDERICK PATTERSON (1871–1932) work with his father, Charles Richard Patterson, who had founded a carriage business, C.R. Patterson & Son Company.

After his father's death, Frederick Patterson developed the Patterson–Greenfield car, making him the first African-American to manufacture cars. Being in direct competition with Henry Ford's Model T, he later converted his business to the Greenfield Bus Body Company.

ANNIE MALONE (1877–1957) was one of America's first and most prominent African-American businesswomen. She founded and developed Poro College, a commercial and educational business focused on cosmetics for black women.

Born to former slaves, Malone developed a chemical that could straighten hair without causing damage to the hair or scalp. Through Poro College, Malone created jobs for 75,000 women around the world. She is recorded as the first black female millionaire in the United States, with a reported $14 million in assets in 1920.

MADAM C.J. WALKER (1867–1919), whose birth name was Sarah Breedlove, attended Annie Malone's Poro College to learn cosmetology. She developed a line of beauty and hair products and is considered one of the first female self-made millionaires in America. Madam C.J. Walker stated:

 • I had to make my own living and my own opportunity ... Don't sit down and wait for the opportunities to come. You have to get up and make them.

• If I have accomplished anything in this life it is because I was willing to work hard.

• I am a woman who came from the cotton fields of the South. From there I was promoted to the washtub. From there I was promoted to the cook kitchen. And from there I promoted myself into the business of manufacturing hair goods and preparations ... I have built my own factory on my own ground.

• I am not merely satisfied in making money for myself, for I am endeavoring to provide employment for hundreds of women of my race.

• I want you to understand your first duty is to humanity. I want others to look at us and see that we care not just about ourselves but about others.

• Its pretty hard for the Lord to guide you if you haven't made up your mind which way to go.

ℭℛ

THE GILDED AGE

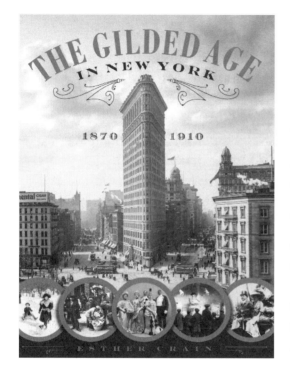

The Industrial Revolution led to manufacturers producing items like clothes, glass, dishes, and farm tools for a fraction of the previous costs. Machines freed women up from tedious daily tasks, such as hand-weaving thread, hand-sewing cloth, and hand-washing clothes.

Instead of carrying water from a well, pumps and pipes brought water directly into homes. New ways of making stronger iron and steel led to the building of bridges, skyscrapers, steamboats, and mining machinery.

Railroads began taking people safely and inexpensively across the entire nation, opening up unprecedented mobility and opportunity. Inventions and advances in manufacturing made more goods available at cheaper prices.

This resulted in Americans experiencing the fastest increase in the standard of living of any people in world history.

This period of American history was called the "Gilded Age" by Mark Twain, with:
- Steam ships crossing the oceans;
- Immigrants arriving from Europe in record numbers;

• Iron and steel production rising dramatically;

• Industry and manufacturing expanded;

• Railroads crossing the nation, with the First Transcontinental Railroad officially completed May 10, 1869;

• Western resources of lumber, cattle, gold and silver;

• Oil industry that saved the whale – as the drilling of oil wells replaced the hunting of whales for blubber to make oil, thus saving whales from being hunted to extinction.

Though sometimes referred to as "Robber Barons," industrialist helped the average person acquire more goods at cheaper prices, resulting in the fastest rise in the "standard of living" of any people in history. Industrialists included:

• John Jacob Astor (real estate, fur);

• Andrew Carnegie (steel);

• James Fisk (finance);

• Henry Flagler (railroads, oil);

• Jay Gould (railroads);

• Edward Harriman (railroads);

• Andrew Mellon (finance, oil);

• J.P. Morgan (finance, industrial);

• John D. Rockefeller (oil);

• Charles M. Schwab (steel); and

• Cornelius Vanderbilt (water transport, railroads).

With the amassing of great wealth also came big business globalist monopolies which attempted to eliminate competition and buy political favors. Unfortunately, President Ulysses S. Grant's military training of trusting subordinates left him ill-prepared for political intrigues, hidden motives and greed of Washington lobbyists.

As a result, several in his Administration were involved in granting government favors, monopolies, "pork" and crony-capitalism kickbacks in exchange for votes, bribes and insider deals. Grant did not personally profit from having been in public office.

Shortly after serving as President, Grant went on a world tour, till he began to show signs of being ill. He had developing throat cancer from his habit of cigar smoking.

Naively trusting investors, Grant went bankrupt, though he insisted on repaying his debts. He was faced with the thought of dying and leaving his wife, Julia, destitute. Mark Twain encouraged him to write his *Memoirs of the Civil War* which provided an income for his wife after his death.

Encouraged by the outpouring of support from across the country, Ulysses S. Grant, who was a Methodist, wrote in 1884:

> I believe in the Holy Scriptures, and whoso lives by them will be benefited thereby. Men may differ as to the interpretation, which is human, but the Scriptures are man's best guide ...

> I did not go riding yesterday, although invited and permitted by my physicians, because it was the Lord's day, and because I felt that if a relapse should set in, the

people who are praying for me would feel that I was not helping their faith by riding out on Sunday ...

Yes, I know, and I feel very grateful to the Christian people of the land for their prayers in my behalf. There is no sect or religion, as shown in the Old or New Testament, to which this does not apply.

Just days after delivering his final manuscript to the printer, Grant died, July 23, 1885. Nine years before he died, Grant gave his views on education to the Editor of *The Sunday School Times* in Philadelphia, June 6, 1876:

Your favor of yesterday asking a message from me to the children and the youth of the United States, to accompany your Centennial number, is this morning received. My advice to Sunday schools, no matter what their denomination, is:

Hold fast to the Bible as the sheet anchor of your liberties; write its precepts in your hearts, and practice them in your lives.

To the influence of this Book are we indebted for all the progress made in true civilization, and to this must we look as our guide in the future. "Righteousness exalteth a nation; but sin is a reproach to any people."

Yours respectfully, U.S. Grant.

ℭℜ

THE STATUE OF LIBERTY WELCOMING THOSE SEEKING TO BE AMERICANS

Factories had a continual source of workers from the millions of immigrants, who not only got a job, but learned the language and trade skills. Immigrants were anxious to assimilate, learn the English language, and swear allegiance to their new country.

"Rags-to-riches" stories, such as those of author Horatio Algiers, Jr., became a popular literary genre, where poor immigrants, through hard work, honesty, and strength in adversity, became successful. Immigrants were not a financial burden on the government, as there were no government welfare programs. Extended family members, churches, and individuals giving charity, provided the welfare net.

To welcome immigrants, President Grover Cleveland dedicated The Statue of Liberty Enlightening the World,

October 28, 1886. He later instituted Labor Day in 1894.

A gift from France, it weighs 450,000 lbs, and stands on a pedestal base, rising 305 feet from the ground to the top of its torch.

Earlier immense statues in history having symbolic meaning were:

• the Colossus of Rhodes – one of the Seven Wonders of the Ancient World; and

• the Colossus of Nero, from which the nearby amphitheater in Rome took its name – Colosseum, both statues being over 100 feet high.

French sculptor Frédéric-Auguste Bartholdi spent two years designing an earlier version of the Statue of Liberty to stand as a lighthouse to guide ships to the entrance of the French built Suez Canal, completed in 1869. Unfortunately, Ismail Pasha, the Khedive (Viceroy) of Egypt and Sudan, could not afford it.

The Statue of Liberty given to America, designed by Frédéric-Auguste Bartholdi, was constructed by Gustave Eiffel, the builder of the Eiffel Tower. Bartholdi wrote:

> The statue was born for this place which inspired its conception. May God be pleased to bless my efforts and my work, and to crown it with success, the duration and the moral influence which it ought to have.

At the Statue's dedication ceremony, Reverend Richard S. Storrs prayed:

> Our Heavenly Father ... by whose counsel and might the courses of the worlds are wisely ordained and irresistibly established ... We bless and praise Thee ... It is in Thy favor, and through the operation of the Gospel of Thy Grace, that cities stand in quiet prosperity; that peaceful commerce covers the seas ...

We pray that the Liberty which it represents may continue ... for all the nations of the earth; that in equity and charity their sure foundations may be established ... that they may be ever the joyful servants of Him to whose holy dominion and kingdom shall be no end.

Dwight Eisenhower remarked April 8, 1954:

I have just come from ... the dedication of a new stamp ... The stamp has on it a picture of the Statue of Liberty and "In God We Trust" ...

It represents ... a Nation whose greatness is based on a firm unshakeable belief that all of us mere mortals are dependent upon the mercy of a Superior Being.

Franklin Roosevelt spoke welcoming those legally immigrating and desiring to assimilate, October 17, 1939:

Remembering the words written on the Statue of Liberty, let us lift a lamp beside new golden doors and build new refuges for the tired, for the poor, for the huddled masses yearning to be free.

In the pedestal of the Statue of Liberty, on a bronze plaque, is the poem "The New Colossus," written in 1883 by the American Jewish poet Emma Lazarus:

Not like the brazen giant of Greek fame,

With conquering limbs astride from land to land;

Here at our sea-washed, sunset gates shall stand

A mighty woman with a torch, whose flame

Is the imprisoned lightning, and her name

Mother of Exiles. From her beacon-hand

Glows world-wide welcome; her mild eyes command

The air-bridged harbor that twin cities frame.

"Keep, ancient lands, your storied pomp!" cries she

With silent lips. "Give me your tired, your poor,

Your huddled masses yearning to breathe free,

The wretched refuse of your teeming shore.

Send these, the homeless, tempest-tost to me,

I lift my lamp beside the golden door!

Emma Lazarus' poem of inspired Rose Hawthorne Lathrop, the daughter of American poet Nathanial Hawthorne, to found the Dominican Sisters of Hawthorne in 1900 to care for those dying of cancer. Lazarus' poem was turned into a song in the 1949 musical "Miss Liberty," composed by Irving Berlin, the Jewish composer of "God Bless America."

On the Statue of Liberty's 50th Anniversary, October 28, 1936, Franklin Roosevelt stated:

Millions … adopted this homeland because … the things they most desired could
be theirs – freedom of opportunity, freedom of thought, freedom to worship God …

FDR added:

Rulers ... increase their power over the common men. The seamen they sent to find that gold found instead the way of escape for the common man from those rulers. What they found over the Western horizon was not the silk and jewels of Cathay but mankind's second chance – a chance to create a new world after he had almost spoiled an old one. The Almighty seems purposefully to have withheld that second chance until the time when men would most need and appreciate liberty ...

FDR continued:

For over three centuries a steady stream of men, women and children followed the beacon of liberty ... They brought to us strength and moral fiber developed in a civilization centuries old but fired anew by the dream of a better life ... The overwhelming majority of those who came from ... the Old World to our American shores were not the laggards, not the timorous, not the failures ...

Franklin D Roosevelt ended:

They were men and women who had the supreme courage to strike out for themselves, to abandon language and relatives, to start at the bottom without influence, without money ... Perhaps Providence did prepare this American continent to be a place of the second chance.

Relighting the Statue of Liberty, July 3, 1986, Ronald Reagan said:

I've always thought that a Providential Hand had something to do with the founding of this country, that God had His reasons for placing this land here between two great oceans to be found by a certain kind of people.

John Adams wrote in his notes on *A Dissertation on the Canon and Feudal Law,* 1765:

I always consider the settlement of America with reverence and wonder, as the opening of a grand scene and design in Providence for the illumination of the ignorant, and the emancipation of the slavish part of mankind all over the earth.

President John F. Kennedy proclaimed October 28, 1961:

We give thanks ... for the heritage of liberty bequeathed by our ancestors which we are privileged to preserve for our children and our children's children ...

I ask the head of each family to recount to his children the story of the first New England Thanksgiving, thus to impress upon future generations the heritage of this nation born in toil, in danger, in purpose, and in the conviction that right and justice and freedom can through man's efforts persevere and come to fruition with the blessing of God.

Ralph Waldo Emerson wrote:

America is another name for opportunity. Our whole history appears like a last effort of Divine Providence in behalf of the human race.

❧

INNOVATIVE BLACK EDUCATORS

Booker T. Washington (1856–1915) was one of the most significant figures in post-Reconstruction America. While he was never technically an entrepreneur, his life work was committed to advancing the educational and economic position of blacks in the United States.

He authored 14 books, such as *Up From Slavery*, which continues to be widely read today. Through his work, he established deep relationships with renowned entrepreneurs and philanthropists, including Andrew Carnegie, John D. Rockefeller, George Eastman, and William Howard Taft; these connections allowed him to funnel huge donations to several initiatives and programs aimed at educating African-Americans.

He also founded the National Negro Business League. Booker T. Washington stated:

> Anyone can seek a job, but it requires a person of rare ability to create a job ... What we should do in our schools is to turn out fewer job seekers and more job creators.

At Memorial Hall in Columbus, Ohio, May 24, 1900, Booker T. Washington delivered an address, "The Place of the Bible in the Uplifting of the Negro Race":

The men doing the vital things of life are those who read the Bible and are Christians and not ashamed to let the world know it ... No man can read the Bible and be lazy.

In the Spring of 1896, Booker T. Washington invited George Washington Carver to teach in Alabama:

Tuskegee Institute seeks to provide education – a means for survival to those who attend. Our students are poor, often starving. They travel miles of torn roads, across years of poverty.

We teach them to read and write, but words cannot fill stomachs. They need to learn how to plant and harvest crops ... I cannot offer you money, position or fame. The first two you have. The last, from the place you now occupy, you will no doubt achieve.

These things I now ask you to give up. I offer you in their place work – hard, hard work – the challenge of bringing people from degradation, poverty and waste to full manhood.

On May 16, 1896, George W. Carver responded to Booker T. Washington:

My dear Sir, I am just in receipt of yours of the 13th inst., and hasten to reply. I am looking forward to a very busy, pleasant and profitable time at your college and shall be glad to cooperate with you in doing all I can through Christ who strengtheneth me to better the condition of our people.

Some months ago I read your stirring address delivered at Chicago and I said amen to all you said, furthermore you have the correct solution to the "race problem" ... Providence permitting, I will be there in November. God bless you and your work, Geo. W. Carver.

Booker T. Washington's solution of the "race problem" was to gain respect through economic independence – the path taken by every wave of immigrants, i.e., German, Irish, Jewish, Polish, Italian, Asian, and others.

Immigrants arrived at the bottom of the social ladder and were often met with racial discrimination. They would work hard, get educated, start businesses, and pool their resources. As they accumulated wealth and made positive contributions to society, they rose in public respect.

Booker T. Washington stated:

At the bottom ... there must be for our race, as for all races ... economic prosperity, economic independence ... Political independence disappears without economic independence.

He recommended they:

... concentrate all their energies on industrial education, and accumulation of wealth, and the conciliation of the South ... (then) Blacks would eventually gain full participation in society by showing themselves to be responsible, reliable American citizens.

GEORGE WASHINGTON CARVER (1864?–1943) was born a slave during the Civil War. He worked to put himself through school, eventually earning a Masters Degree from Iowa State in Agriculture. He accepted Booker T. Washington's invitation to teach at Tuskegee Institute.

Carver is credited with discovering and/or popularizing hundreds of uses for the peanut, soybean, sweet potato, pecan, cowpea, wild plum, and okra, which helped to revolutionize the South's economy. He addressed Congress and met with Presidents Teddy Roosevelt, Calvin Coolidge and Franklin Roosevelt.

He was offered jobs by Henry Ford and Thomas Edison and received correspondence from business and world leaders. In 1939, he was awarded the Roosevelt Medal, with the declaration:

> To a scientist humbly seeking the guidance of God and a liberator to men of the white race as well as the black.

In 1928, Dr. George Washington Carver explained:

> Human need is really a great spiritual vacuum which God seeks to fill ... With one hand in the hand of a fellow man in need and the other in the hand of Christ, He could get across the vacuum ...

> Then the passage, "I can do all things through Christ which strengthens me," came to have real meaning.

Edward Alexander Bouchet (1852–1918) was the first African American to earn a doctorate degree in the United States. Son of a former slave, he studied history, Latin, Greek, chemistry, and mathematics at Hopkins Grammar School in New Haven, Connecticut, where he graduated valedictorian in 1870.

At Yale, he earned a bachelor's degree, then a doctorate in physics in 1876. He served as a deacon at Temple Street Church in New Haven.

In Philadelphia, Bouchet taught at the School for Colored Youth and was a lay reader at St. Thomas African Episcopal Church.

He taught in St. Louis, Missouri, at Charles Sumner High School, named for the famous abolitionist Senator, and at St. Paul Normal and Industrial School in Virginia.

He was principal of Lincoln High School, and was a faculty member at Bishop College in Marshall, Texas, founded by the Baptist Home Mission Society in 1881.

In his honor, Yale gives the Bouchet Leadership Award, established the Edward Alexander Bouchet Graduate Honor Society and the Graduate School of Arts and Sciences in his name.

‍ CR

PANAMA CANAL

Canal construction has spanned history:

• Mesopotamia and India had the oldest canals for irrigation, c. 3,000 BC;

• China's Grand Canal, begun in the 5th century BC, is almost 1,800 miles, linking the Yellow River and the Yangtze River;

• Greeks engineered canals, c 400 BC;

• Romans built extensive canals, pipes, tunnels, aqueducts & bridges, 312 BC–226 AD;

• Charlemagne oversaw in 793 AD the first artificial canal in Western Europe at Fossa Carolina, from the Rhine River basin to the Danube River basin;

• Britain's Glastonbury Canal was built in the 10th century;

• Italy's Naviglio Canal from the Ticino River to Milan took a century to complete, 1157–1258;

• England's Exeter Canal was constructed in the 1560s;

• Netherlands, Flanders & Belgium constructed a dense system of canals, mostly in the 1600s;

• France's Canal de Briare, connecting the Loire and Seine Valleys, was completed in 1642;

• Germans built 18th century canals on rivers Spree, Elbe, Havel, Ems, Elster, Dahme, Oder, Weser;

• Russia's canals were pioneered by Peter the Great, who built the Vyshny Volochyok Waterway, 1703–1722, connecting Saint Petersburg with the Baltic Sea, and later expanded in the 19th century to the White Sea;

• United States completed the 363 mile long Erie Canal in 1827, from Albany to Buffalo.

The idea of crossing the Isthmus of Panama began when Columbus first landed there in October 6, 1502, during his fourth and final voyage. In 1534, the King of Spain, Charles V, who ruled the first global empire, ordered a survey of the Isthmus of Panama to assess the feasibility of a canal.

Such a canal would save explorers and merchants from having to sail the long, dangerous route around South America, passing through the Strait of Magellan, first traversed by Ferdinand Magellan in 1520.

A canal across Panama was again suggested in 1658 by England's Sir Thomas Browne.

In 1698, the Kingdom of Scotland attempted the Darien scheme, a trade colony in Panama to connect the Atlantic and Pacific Oceans. Unfortunately for them, it was financially suppressed by the British East India Company and obstructed by a Spanish blockade.

Thomas Jefferson suggested a canal there in 1788.

From 1788 to 1793, a Spanish naval officer, Alessandro Malaspina, sailed around the world and explored the Pacific. He also proposed an outline for construction plans for a canal.

In 1827, Simón Bolívar, President of La Gran Colombia (Venezuela, Ecuador, Panama,

Colombia), studied the feasibility of a railway across the Isthmus, as did U.S. President Andrew Jackson in 1836.

In 1838, a French company attempted to build a railroad and canal route, but it failed for lack of funding and technology.

In 1846, the U.S. signed a treaty with New Granada (Colombia) for rights to build a rail or canal route.

After the Mexican–American War, 1848, and the California Gold Rush, 1849, Captain Ulysses S. Grant and the 4th Infantry were ordered to relocate to San Francisco, traveling by way of Panama in 1852. While crossing the Isthmus, a cholera epidemic killed so many soldiers that Grant organized a field hospital and cared for the ill himself, writing:

> The horrors of the road in the rainy season are beyond description.

The Panama Railroad Company, formed by New York businessmen, began building the first transcontinental railroad from the Atlantic to the Pacific. Construction workers were English, Irish, Germans, Africans, Caribbean, Indian, and Chinese. Completed in 1855, the nearly 50 mile railroad across muddy insect-infested, disease-ridden swamps, cost over 5,000 lives.

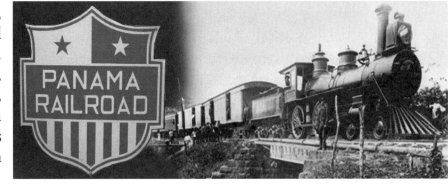

Mark Twain wrote a Special Correspondence of the Chicago Republican, New York, August 17, 1868:

> The Panama railroad was an American project ... We took the train at Panama, clattered for two or three hours through a tangled wilderness of tropical vegetation, and discharged ourselves in Aspinwall (Colón). It is only forty-five miles ...
>
> That little road has carried about 100,000 passengers for the California steamers during the past twelve months ... It was a hard road to build. The tropical fevers slaughtered the laborers by wholesale.
>
> It is a popular saying, that every railroad tie from Panama to Aspinwall rests upon a corpse ... It is claimed that this small railroad enterprise cost the lives of 10,000 men. It is possible.

The idea for the Panama Canal gained momentum when the French finished the 120–mile–long Suez Canal in 1869.

The construction of the Suez Canal was led by builder Ferdinand de Lesseps. It roughly followed the path of an ancient canal built by King Darius of Persia in the 5th century BC. The Suez Canal enabled ships from the Far East and the Indian Ocean to reach the Mediterranean Sea without having to sail around the continent of Africa.

French sculptor Frédéric-Auguste Bartholdi spent two years designing an earlier version of the Statue of Liberty to stand as a lighthouse to guide ships to the entrance of the Suez Canal, but Ismail Pasha, the Khedive (Viceroy) of Egypt and Sudan, could not afford it.

In 1880, France's Ferdinand de Lesseps began building a sea-level canal across the Isthmus of Panama. France's efforts were hindered by torrential seasonal rains which caused massive landslides. France eventually abandoned the project due to the tropical diseases of malaria and yellow fever, which killed 25,000.

In 1899, a U.S. Army physician, Dr. Walter Reed, went to Cuba after

the Spanish–American War do research. He scientifically confirmed the previous discovery of Dr. Carlos Finlay, that malaria and yellow fever were carried by mosquitoes.

This knowledge led to efforts of public sanitation and the development of insecticides which saved thousands of lives and made construction of a canal in Panama possible. Walter Reed Army Medical Center, founded in 1909, was named for him.

On November 3, 1903, the United States aided Panama in gaining independence from Colombia.

Also that year, on December 17, 1903, Wilbur and Orville Wright made the first controlled, sustained flight of a powered, heavier-than-air aircraft four miles south of Kitty Hawk, North

Carolina, introducing the era of air travel.

On February 23, 1904, the United States purchased the Canal Zone from Panama for ten million dollars on February 23, 1904, plus annual payments of $250,000.

The Panama Canal was planned by President William McKinley and construction began under President Theodore Roosevelt.

Instead of a straight sea-level canal, Roosevelt favored a set of three locks rising from sea-level to Gatun Lake, then on the other side of the lake, to have three locks going back down to sea level.

On December 17, 1906, President Theodore Roosevelt told Congress:

> The Isthmus had been a by-word for deadly unhealthfulness. Now, after two years of our occupation the conditions as regards sickness and the death rate compare ... with reasonably healthy localities in the United States.

> Special care has been devoted to minimizing the risk due to the presence of those species of mosquitoes which have been found to propagate malarial and yellow fevers.

Advances in pesticides helped save millions of lives, with 5 of the 11 Nobel Prizes awarded between 1939 and 1952 going to scientists who made advances in controlling the spread of diseases.

Though used to eradicate mosquito-borne diseases in wealthier nations, the most effective pesticides were banned before they could do the same in Africa.

Similarly, the Space program giving birth to new technologies, construction of the

Panama Canal birthed many inventions , such as:
- railroad innovations; • steam shovels;
- steam-powered cranes; • hydraulic rock crushers;
- cement mixers; • dredges;
- drilling machinery; • pneumatic power drills; and
- massive electric motors.

These inventions were largely developed and built in the United States. They were used to create Panama's Gatun Lake – the largest dam and man-made lake in the world at that time.

President William Taft addressed Congress, December 6, 1912:

> Our defense of the Panama Canal, together with our enormous world trade and our missionary outposts on the frontiers of civilization, require us to recognize our position as one of the foremost in the family of nations, and to clothe ourselves with sufficient naval power to give force to our reasonable demands, and to give weight to our influence in those directions of progress that a powerful Christian nation should advocate.

On October 23, 1913, President Wilson stated:

> We have seen the practical completion of a great work at the Isthmus of Panama which not only exemplifies the nation's abundant capacity of its public servants but also promises the

beginning of a new age of co-operation and peace. "Righteousness exalteth a nation" and "peace on earth, good will towards men" furnish the only foundation upon which can be built the lasting achievements of the human spirit.

The Panama Canal was opened August 15, 1914, the same year World War I began. Within 10 years, more than 5,000 ships a year were passing through the Panama Canal.

The largest American engineering project to that date, it had cost the United States $375,000,000 (over $10 billion today). The Panama Canal also cost 5,600 American lives, over 100 for every one of the 50 miles across the Isthmus.

On March 31, 1976, California Governor Ronald Reagan stated:

> Well, the Canal Zone is not a colonial possession. It is not a long-term lease. It is sovereign United States Territory every bit the same as Alaska and all the states that were carved from the Louisiana Purchase ... We bought it, we paid for it, we built it, and we intend to keep it.

After contentious public debate, Democrat President Jimmy Carter gave away the Panama Canal in 1977. Concern arose as to what international influences would fill the vacuum once the United States transferred control.

Such concern was voiced by Admiral Thomas Moorer, commander of the U.S. Pacific and Atlantic fleets and Chairman of the Joint Chiefs of Staff from 1970 to 1974, who stated in *The New American*, March 29, 1999:

> Chinese are poised to effectively take control of the Panama Canal ... The Panama Canal is very close to home and is one of our most vital commercial and military assets ... In 1996, while China was illegally pouring millions of dollars into Clinton's reelection effort, it was also funneling huge amounts of cash to Panamanian politicians to ensure that one of its front companies, Hutchison Whampoa of Hong Kong, could move in when we vacate ...

Moorer continued:

> In 1997, Panama secretly turned over the American-built port facility at Balboa, which controls shipping on the Pacific side, and at Cristobal, which controls shipping on the Atlantic side, to Hutchison ... We are scheduled to turn over Rodman Naval Station, Howard Air Force Base, and other important military facilities to Panama, which has given Hutchison an option on these bases ...

Admiral Moorer concluded:

> President Clinton may say that they are our friends and allies, but the Chinese military and Communist Party literature refer to the United States as "the main enemy." And despite what ... Henry Kissinger, and the media may tell you about

"reform" in China, it is still run by a brutal, totalitarian, Communist regime that will do us harm if and when it thinks it can get the better of us.

China's Hutchinson Ports (CK Hutchinson Holdings) is the world's largest seaport operator. In addition to controlling U.S. built anchor ports on either end of the Panama Canal (Balboa and Cristobal), it controls strategic ports all around the globe.

Panama has been a popular haven for American expats who prefer to not live in the United States, as it has warm climate, beautiful scenery, the cost-of-living is financially favorable. For safety, though, it is not uncommon to see bars on windows, fences, walls and armed security.

Since the mid–1970s, Panama, along with other Central and South American countries, has experienced Muslim immigration, with El Centro Cultural Islámico de Colón being dedicated on January 15, 1982. The publication CRITICA reported (9/16/15) "ISIS Amenaza a Panama" (ISIS Threat to Panama.)

In 2016, the Panama Canal opened a new set of locks, doubling the waterway's capacity to accommodate larger ships.

An American-built canal, President Theodore Roosevelt wrote in his Autobiography:

> By far the most important action I took in foreign affairs during the time I was President was related to the Panama Canal

ॐ

SCOPES MONKEY TRIAL & WILLIAM JENNINGS BRYAN

The Scopes Monkey Trial in 1925 pitted evolution against creation. Clarence Darrow was the attorney who defended evolution.

He had previously defended Leopold and Loeb, the teenage homosexual thrill killers who murdered 14-year-old Robert "Bobby" Franks in 1924 just for the excitement.

Darrow obtained a pardon for antifa-type anarchists in 1886 who blew up a pipe bomb in Chicago's Haymarket Square, killing 7 policemen and injured 60 others. A Haymarket Statue was dedicated to the fallen policemen, but in 1969 it was blown up by socialist anarchists "Weather Underground" prior to their "Days of Rage" protests. The statue was rebuilt, but blown up again in 1970. The Weather Underground had a lasting impact, with two leaders, Bill Ayers and Bernadine Dohrn, hosting a 1995 meeting to help launch the political career of an Illinois State Senator who later ran for President; and another leader, Eric Mann, who trained Patrisse Cullors, a founder of a well-funded protest organization.

Clarence Darrow defended the "mentally deranged drifter" Patrick Eugene Prendergast in 1894 who confessed to murdering Chicago mayor Carter H. Harrison, Sr.

Darrow defended socialist organizer Eugene V. Debs, who was prosecuted for instigating the Pullman Railroad Strike which caused 30 deaths, 57 wounded, and $80 million in property damages in 27 states. Debs founded the Socialist Party of America, which branched off the Communist Party USA in 1919.

Darrow represented the Western Federation of Miners leaders charged with the 1905 murder of former Idaho Gov. Frank Steunenberg. In 1911, the American Federation of Labor arranged for Darrow to defend the McNamara brothers. The McNamara brothers were charged with dynamiting *The Los Angeles Times* building which killed 21 employees.

Implicated in bribing jurors, Darrow was banned from practicing law in California.

In 1925, Darrow unsuccessfully defended John Scopes, a Tennessee high school biology teacher who taught the theory of origins called "evolution." The attorney defending creation was the Democrat Party's three time candidate for President, William Jennings Bryan. He objected to a tooth being presented as proof of humans evolving from apes. Later the tooth was found to be that of an extinct peccary (pig).

William Jennings Bryan won the Scopes case on July 21, 1925. Though Darrow lost, a pro-evolution propaganda film was produced in 1960 titled *Inherit the Wind*.

Professor Alan M. Dershowitz wrote on "The Scopes Trial" in his book *America on Trial: Inside the Legal Battles that Transformed Our Nation* (eBook Edition: May 2004):

> The popular perception of what transpired in the courtroom comes not from the transcript of the court proceeding itself, but rather from the motion picture ...

Inherit the Wind. The William Jennings Bryan character, Scopes's prosecutor, was a burlesque of know-nothing religious literalism ... The actual William Jennings Bryan was no simple-minded literalist, and he certainly was no bigot. He was a great populist who cared deeply about equality and about the downtrodden.

Indeed, one of his reasons for becoming so deeply involved in the campaign against evolution was that Darwin's theories were being used – misused, it turns out – by racists, militarists, and nationalists to further some pretty horrible programs ...

Dershowitz continued:

The eugenics movement, which advocated sterilization of "unfit" and "inferior" stock, was at its zenith, and it took its impetus from Darwin's theory of natural selection. German militarism, which had just led to the disastrous world war, drew inspiration from Darwin's ideas on survival of the fittest.

The anti-immigration movement, which had succeeded in closing American ports of entry to "inferior racial stock," was grounded in a mistaken belief that certain ethnic groups had evolved more fully than others ...

The Jim Crow laws, which maintained racial segregation, were rationalized on grounds of the racial inferiority of blacks. Indeed, the very book – *Hunter's Civic Biology* – from which John T. Scopes taught Darwin's theory of evolution to high school students in Dayton, Tennessee, contained dangerous misapplications of that theory ...

Dershowitz added:

Indeed, its very title, *Civic Biology*, made it clear that biology had direct political implications for civic society. In discussing the "five races" of man, the text assured the all-white, legally segregated high school students taught by Scopes that "the highest type of all, the Caucasians, (are) represented by the civilized white inhabitants of Europe and America." The book, the avowed goal of which was the improvement of the future human race, then proposed certain eugenic remedies.

Eugenic laws, based on evolution, were passed in many states. Virginia's eugenic law, in 1924, allowed for the state to sterilize its first victim, Carrie Buck, who was a patient in the State Colony for Epileptics and Feeble-minded.

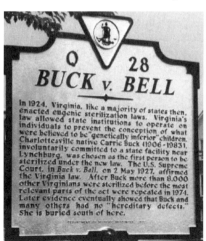

A case was brought which went to the Supreme Court. There, Justice Oliver Wendell Holmes, Jr., gave his infamous *Buck v. Bell* decision in 1927 which continued to allow the sterilization of people without their knowledge or consent, stating: "Three generations of imbeciles are enough."

Because of Holmes' decision, Virginia continued to sterilize more than 8,000 people until the practice was stopped in 1974. Holmes also applied evolution to his decision-making philosophy, calling it "legal realism," letting judges alter laws to adapt to changing social and economic conditions.

Professor Alan Dershowitz continued his critique of the high school textbook used by John Scopes, *Hunter's Civic Biology*:

After a discussion of the inheritability of crime and immorality, the author proposed an analogy: ... "Just as certain animals or plants become parasitic on other plants or animals, these families have become parasitic on society. They not only do harm to others by corrupting, stealing, or spreading disease, but they are actually protected and cared for by the state out of public money ... They take from society, but they give nothing in return. They are true parasites ..."

Dershowitz added:

From the analogy flowed "the remedy": "If such people were lower animals, we would probably kill them off to prevent them from spreading.

Humanity will not allow this, but we do have the remedy of separating the sexes in asylums or other places and in various ways preventing intermarriage and the possibilities of perpetuating such a low and degenerate race. Remedies of this sort have been tried successfully in Europe and are now meeting with success in this country."

These "remedies" included involuntary sterilizations, and eventually laid the foundation for involuntary "euthanasia" of the kind practiced in Nazi Germany ...

Dershowitz continued:

Nor were these misapplications of Darwinian theory limited to high school textbooks. Eugenic views held sway at institutions of higher learning such as Harvard University, under racist president Abbot Lawrence Lowell.

Even so distinguished a Supreme Court justice as Oliver Wendell Holmes upheld

a mandatory sterilization law on the basis of a pseudo-scientific assumption about heritability and genetics. His widely quoted rationale – that "three generations of imbeciles are enough" – was later cited by Nazi apologists for mass sterilization ...

It should not be surprising, therefore, that William Jennings Bryan ... would be outraged – both morally and religiously ... The textbook Scopes wanted to teach was ... a bad science text, filled with misapplied Darwinism and racist rubbish.

G.K. Chesterton wrote in *The Everlasting Man*, 1925:

Nobody can imagine how nothing could turn into something. Nobody can get an inch nearer to it by explaining how something could turn into something else. It is really far more logical to start by saying "In the beginning God created heaven and earth:" even if you only mean "In the beginning some unthinkable power began some unthinkable process."

For God is by its nature a name of mystery, and nobody ever supposed that man could imagine how a world was created any more than he could create one. But evolution really is mistaken for explanation. It has the fatal quality of leaving on many minds the impression that they do understand it and everything else

After the trial, William Jennings Bryan wrote in his summary of the Scopes trial of how science tells us what we can do, religion tells us what we should do:

Science is a magnificent force, but it is not a teacher of morals. It can perfect machinery, but it adds no moral restraints to protect society from the misuse of the machine.

It can also build gigantic intellectual ships, but it constructs no moral rudders for the control of storm-tossed human vessel. It not only fails to supply the spiritual element needed but some of its unproven hypotheses rob the ship of its compass and thus endanger its cargo ...

Bryan continued:

In war, science has proven itself an evil genius; it has made war more terrible than it ever was before. Man used to be content to slaughter his fellowmen on a single plane, the earth's surface.

Science has taught him to go down into the water and shoot up from below and to go up into the clouds and shoot down from above, thus making the battlefield three times as bloody as it was before; but science does not teach brotherly love.

Science has made war so hellish that civilization was about to commit suicide; and now we are told that newly discovered instruments of destruction will make the cruelties of the late war seem trivial in comparison with the cruelties of wars that may come in the future ...

Bryan concluded:

> If civilization is to be saved from the wreckage threatened by intelligence not consecrated by love, it must be saved by the moral code of the meek and lowly Nazarene. His teachings, and His teachings alone, can solve the problems that vex the heart and perplex the world.

Bryan's 1925 statement was echoed by Winston Churchill, who stated in 1941:

> But if we fail, then the whole world, including the United States ... will sink into the abyss of a new Dark Age made more sinister, and perhaps more protracted, by the lights of perverted science.

Science tells us what we *can* do – religion tells us what we *should* do. In 1909, Theodore Roosevelt had warned:

> The thought of modern industry in the hands of Christian charity is a dream worth dreaming. The thought of industry in the hands of paganism is a nightmare beyond imagining. The choice between the two is upon us.

William Jennings Bryan had been a Colonel in the Spanish–American War, a U.S. Representative from Nebraska and U.S. Secretary of State under Democrat President Woodrow Wilson. He edited the *Omaha World Herald* and founded *The Commoner Newspaper*.

Dying five days after the Scopes Trial, William Jennings Bryan was so popular that his statue was placed in the U.S. Capitol's Statuary Hall by the State of Nebraska and the Post Office issued a $2.00 stamp in his honor.

Bryan gave over 600 public speeches during his campaigns. His most famous was "The Prince of Peace," *New York Times*, September 7, 1913, in which he stated:

> I am interested in the science of government but I am more interested in religion ... I enjoy making a political speech ... but I would rather speak on religion than on politics. I commenced speaking on the stump when I was only twenty, but I commenced speaking in the church six years earlier – and I shall be in the church even after I am out of politics ...

Bryan reasoned:

> Tolstoy ... declares that the religious sentiment rests not upon a superstitious fear ... but upon man's consciousness of his finiteness amid an infinite universe ... Man feels the weight of his sins and looks for One who is sinless. Religion has been defined by Tolstoy as the relation which man fixes between himself and his God ... Religion is the foundation of morality in the individual and in the group of individuals ...

> A religion which teaches personal responsibility to God gives strength to morality. There is a powerful restraining influence in the belief that an all-seeing eye scrutinizes every thought and word and act of the individual ... One needs the inner strength which comes with the conscious presence of a personal God ...

Bryan stated further:

I passed through a period of skepticism when I was in college ... The college days cover the dangerous period in the young man's life; he is just coming into possession of his powers, and feels stronger than he ever feels afterward – and he thinks he knows more than he ever does know.

It was at this period that I became confused by the different theories of creation. But I examined these theories and found that they all assumed something to begin with ... A Designer back of the design – a Creator back of the creation; and no matter how long you draw out the process of creation, so long as God stands back of it you cannot shake my faith in Jehovah ...

We must begin with something – we must start somewhere – and the Christian begins with God ...

Bryan continued:

While you may trace your ancestry back to the monkey ... you shall not connect me with your family tree ... The ape, according to this theory, is older than man and yet the ape is still an ape while man is the author of the marvelous civilization which we see about us ...

This theory ... does not explain the origin of life. When the follower of Darwin has traced the germ of life back to the lowest form ... to follow him one must exercise more faith than religion calls for ...

Bryan explained:

Those who reject the idea of creation are divided into two schools, some believing that the first germ of life came from another planet and others holding that it was the result of spontaneous generation ... Go back as far as we may, we cannot escape from the creative act, and it is just as easy for me to believe that God created man as he is as to believe that, millions of years ago, He created a germ of life and endowed it with power to develop ...

But there is another objection. The Darwinian theory represents man as reaching his present perfection by the operation of the law of hate – the merciless law by which the strong crowd out and kill off the weak ... I prefer to believe that love rather than hatred is the law of development ...

William Jennings Bryan concluded:

Science has disclosed some of the machinery of the universe, but science has not yet revealed to us the great secret – the secret of life. It is to be found in every blade of grass, in every insect, in every bird and in every animal, as well as in man.

Six thousand years of recorded history and yet we know no more about the secret of life than they knew in the beginning ... If the Father deigns to touch with divine power the cold and pulseless heart of the buried acorn and to make it burst forth from its prison walls, will he leave neglected in the earth the soul of man, made in the image of his Creator? ... The Gospel of the Prince of Peace gives us the only hope that the world has.

Democrat President Franklin Roosevelt stated at the Memorial to William Jennings Bryan, May 3, 1934:

No selfish motive touched his public life; he held important office only as a sacred trust of honor from his country ... To Secretary Bryan political courage was not a virtue to be sought or attained, for it was an inherent part of the man. He chose his path not to win acclaim but rather because that path appeared clear to him from his inmost beliefs. He did not have to dare to do what to him seemed right; he could not do otherwise ...

Roosevelt continued:

It was my privilege to know William Jennings Bryan when I was a very young man. Years later both of us came to the Nation's capital to serve under the leadership of Woodrow Wilson ...

It was Mr. Bryan who said: "I respect the aristocracy of learning, I deplore the plutocracy of wealth but I thank God for the democracy of the heart." Many years ago he also said: "You may dispute over whether I have fought a good fight; you may dispute over whether I have finished my course; but you cannot deny that I have kept the faith."

We who are assembled here today to accept this memorial in the capital of the Republic can well agree that he fought a good fight; that he finished his course; and that he kept the faith.

℃ℛ

DR. ALBERT SCHWEITZER "REVERENCE FOR LIFE"

Albert Schweitzer was born January 14, 1875, in a village in Alsace, Germany. The son of an Evangelical Lutheran pastor, he won acclaim at playing the organ. He earned doctorates in philosophy and theology.

Schweitzer was pastor of St. Nicholas Church. He was also the principal of St. Thomas College and a professor at University of Strasbourg.

Then, at age 30, his life changed. He read a Paris Missionary Society article of the desperate need for physicians in Africa.

To everyone's dismay, he enrolled in medical school and became a medical missionary. In 1912, he married a nurse, Helene Bresslau. With her support, the next year they traveled to west central Africa and founded a hospital in the jungle village of Lambarene, Gabon.

After first using a chicken hut as their medical clinic, they erected a hospital building of corrugated iron in 1913. In the first 9 months they saw over 2,000 patients.

World War I started, and the conflict between France and Germany went global, reaching into Africa. The Schweitzers were arrested and put under French military supervision, then taken to a prison camp in France.

After the war, they moved to Alsace-Lorraine, a border area between France and Germany, where their only child was born, a daughter, Rhena. Saving their money, Helene stayed back with their daughter, Rhena, and Albert returned to Gabon in 1924. Traveling back and forth several times, they rebuilt the hospital.

They served uninterrupted throughout World War II, being joined by additional staff.

The patients they treated suffered from: malaria, fever, dysentery, severe sandflea bites, tropical eating sores, leprosy, crawcraw sores, sleeping sickness, yaws (tropical infection of skin & bones), nicotine poisoning, necrosis, heart disease, chronic constipation, strangulated hernias, and abdominal tumors.

He helped Mbahouin tribes and pygmies who were in fear of being hunted and victims of cannibalism.

Albert Schweitzer spoke in Europe and in 1949 visited the United States. Once he was asked "Why are you traveling in the 4th class?" He replied "Because there is no 5th class."

Once on a train two schoolgirls asked him, "Dr. Einstein, will you give us your autograph?" Not wanting to disappoint them, he signed: "Albert Einstein, by his friend Albert Schweitzer."

His daughter, Rhena, became a medical technician and married an American doctor, David C. Miller, who was serving at the African hospital – Albert Schweitzer Hospital.

Albert Schweitzer joined Albert Einstein in warning the world of the dangers in developing nuclear weapons.

In 1952, Dr. Schweitzer was awarded the Nobel Peace Prize. He used the prize money to build a leper colony. He embraced a pro-life philosophy, explaining:

> For months on end, I lived in a continual state of mental agitation. Without the least success I concentrated – even during my daily work at the hospital – on the real nature of the affirmation of life and of ethics ... I was wandering about in a thicket where no path was to be found. I was pushing against an iron door that would not yield ... In that mental state, I had to take a long journey up the river ...

> Lost in thought, I sat on deck of the barge, struggling to find the elementary and universal concept of the ethical that I had not discovered in any philosophy. I covered sheet after sheet with disconnected sentences merely to concentrate on the problem.

> Two days passed. Late on the third day, at the very moment when, at sunset, we were making our way through a herd of hippopotamuses, there flashed upon my mind,

unforeseen and unsought, the phrase: "Ehrfurcht vor dem Leben" ("Reverence for Life"). The iron door had yielded. The path in the thicket had become visible.

Schweitzer's words stand in contrast to utilitarian cultures and political party platforms advocating euthanasia, organ harvesting, honor-killings, and abortion,

At the beginning of World War II, *The New York Times* reported October 10, 1933, on the utilitarian views of socialized medicine in Germany:

NAZI PLAN TO KILL INCURABLES ... The Ministry of Justice ... explaining the (National Socialist Workers Party) ... intentions to authorize physicians to end the sufferings of the incurable patient ...

The Catholic newspaper *Germania* hastened to observe: "The Catholic faith binds the conscience of its followers not to accept this method" ... In Lutheran circles, too, life is regarded as something that God alone can take ...

Euthanasia ... has become a widely discussed word in the (Third) Reich ... No life still valuable to the State will be wantonly destroyed.

In contrast to this utilitarian view, Dr. Schweitzer stated:

Ethics is nothing other than Reverence for Life. Reverence for Life affords me my fundamental principle of morality, namely, that good consists in maintaining, assisting and enhancing life, and to destroy, to harm or to hinder life is evil.

In declaring National Sanctity of Human Life Day, President Trump said January 22, 2018:

Reverence for every human life, one of the values for which our Founding Fathers fought, defines the character of our Nation. Today, it moves us to promote the health of pregnant mothers and their unborn children.

Schweitzer's attitude was in line with the Hippocratic Oath, which, up until recent times, was taken by all medical practitioners to protect all human life – "First ... do no harm":

> I swear ... I will use those dietary regimens which will benefit my patients according to my greatest ability and judgment, and I will do no harm or injustice to them. I will not give a lethal drug to anyone if I am asked, nor will I advise such a plan; and similarly I will not give a woman a pessary to cause an abortion. In purity and according to divine law will I carry out my life and my art.

Schweitzer wrote in *Indian Thought and Its Development* (1935):

> The laying down of the commandment to not kill and to not damage is one of the greatest events in the spiritual history of mankind.

He wrote in his autobiography *Out of My Life and Thought: An Autobiography* (1931):

> The world-view based on reverence for life is, through the religious character of its ethic of active love and through its fervor, essentially akin to that of Christianity ... What Christianity needs is to be filled with the spirit of Jesus Christ, to become living, intense, a religion of love which it was meant to be.

Since I myself am deeply devoted to Christianity, I seek to serve it with fidelity and truth. I hope that the thought which has resulted in this simple, ethical-religious idea – reverence for life – may help to bring Christianity and thought closer to each other.

Schweitzer's life has been portrayed in numerous documentaries and films, including the 2009 movie *Albert Schweitzer–A Life for Africa*, starring Jeroen Krabbé.

Many groups work to raise awareness of crimes against life, and endeavor to protect it.

• VOICE OF THE MARTYRS documents crimes committed against Christian minorities in Egypt, Iraq, Iran, Syria, Pakistan, Turkey, Palestine, Uzbekistan, South Sudan, Ivory Coast, Tanzania, Indonesia, and Nigeria.

• INTERNATIONAL SOCIETY FOR HUMAN RIGHTS reported that 80 per cent of all acts of religious discrimination in the world today are directed at Christians.

• CENTRE FOR THE STUDY OF GLOBAL CHRISTIANITY estimated that every years 100,000 Christians, 11 every hour, die because of their faith.

• PEW RESEARCH CENTER reported in 2012 that Christians faced discrimination in 139 countries, nearly 3/4s of the nations in the world.

• *THE GLOBAL WAR ON CHRISTIANS* (Random House) author John Allen stated that followers of Jesus are "indisputably ... the most persecuted religious body on the planet."

• *CHRISTIANOPHOBIA: A FAITH UNDER ATTACK* (Eerdmans) author Rupert Shortt reported from Nigeria to the Far East, Christians are targets of violent human rights abuses and intimidation: "in a vast belt of land from Morocco to Pakistan there is scarcely a single country in which Christians can worship entirely without harassment."

• OPEN DOORS USA estimated 100 million Christians are persecuted globally each year, mostly from Islamic extremism. Open Doors president David Curry "Tactics used by the Islamic State are being adopted and used in Africa."

• *WORLD MAGAZINE* reported: "Of the 50 countries most hostile to Christians, Kenya rose on the list more than any other country, jumping to No. 19 ... Sudan (No. 6) and Eritrea (No. 9) ... Nigeria moved into the top 10 for the first time ever ... where more than 2,400 people died for their faith in specific, targeted attacks ... *The Wall Street Journal* reported Boko Haram now controls a swath of land the size of Belgium."

After reading these tragic reports, one is challenged by a sermon of Dr. Albert Schweitzer, January 6, 1905:

Our Christianity – yours and mine – has become a falsehood and a disgrace, if the crimes are not atoned for in the very place where they were instigated ... For every person who committed an atrocity ... someone must step in to help in Jesus' name; for every person who robbed, someone must bring a replacement; for everyone who cursed, someone must bless ...

He continued:

When you speak about missions, let this be your message: We must make atonement for all the terrible crimes we read of in the newspapers. We must make atonement for the still worse ones, which we do not read about in the papers, crimes that are shrouded in the silence of the jungle night.

After his wife died, Dr. Albert Schweitzer continued to work in Africa till his death at age 90. Overcoming innumerable difficulties, he once wrote:

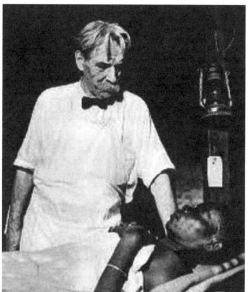

One day, in my despair, I threw myself into a chair in the consulting room and groaned out: "What a blockhead I was to come out here to doctor savages like these!" ... Whereupon his native assistant quietly remarked: "Yes, Doctor, here on earth you are a great blockhead, but not in heaven."

Dr. Albert Schweitzer wrote:

I don't know what your destiny will be, but one thing I do know: the only ones among you who will be really happy are those who have sought and found how to serve.

CR

SANCTITY OF LIFE
"SCIENTIFICALLY CORRECT ...
LIFE BEGINS AT CONCEPTION"

Being interviewed on his book, *Our Enduring Values–America's Moral Crisis*, former Democrat President Jimmy Carter stated at the Ritz-Carlton Hotel, Washington, DC, November 3, 2005:

> I never have felt that any abortion should be committed – I think each abortion is the result of a series of errors ... I've never been convinced, if you let me inject my Christianity into it, that Jesus Christ would approve abortion ... I have always thought it was not in the mainstream of the American public to be extremely liberal on many issues. I think our party's leaders ... are overemphasizing the abortion issue.

A 2020 Democrat candidate for President, Pete Buttigieg, claimed to be "Christian," yet proposed that instead of life beginning at conception, it was "life begins at breath." His belief departs from Christianity, as Christ himself was in his mother's womb at conception.

Jesus, as recorded in the Gospel of Luke, was in Mary's womb from the moment of the Annunciation, when the Angel announced to her, "Behold, you will conceive in your womb and bear a son, and you shall call his name Jesus" and she responded, "Behold the handmaid of the Lord; be it unto me according to thy word."

The Angel continued:

> The Holy Ghost shall come upon thee, and the power of the Highest shall overshadow thee: therefore also that holy thing which shall be born of thee shall be called the Son of God."

At that very instant, she conceived. This is the foundational Christian doctrine called Jesus' Incarnation, when "the Word became flesh." The Gospel of Luke continued with another account confirming that a child in the womb was alive:

> "And behold, your kinswoman Elizabeth in her old age has also conceived a son; and this is the sixth month with her who was called barren" ... When Elisabeth heard the salutation of Mary, the babe leaped in her womb."

Scriptures testify that a baby in the womb is a living person:

> • Genesis 25:21–23 "And Rebekah his wife conceived. And the children struggled together within her; and she said, If it be so, why am I thus? And she went to inquire of the Lord. And the Lord said unto her, Two nations are in thy womb, and two manner of people shall be separated from thy bowels; and the one people shall be stronger than the other people; and the elder shall serve the younger."

- Jeremiah 1:5 "Before I formed you in the womb I knew you, before you were born I set you apart; I appointed you as a prophet to the nations."
- Isaiah 49:1,5 "The LORD called me from the womb, from the body of my mother he named my name ... he who formed me from the womb to be his servant, to bring Jacob back to him."
- Psalm 22:10 "Thou art my God from my mother's belly."
- Galatians 1:15 "He who had set me apart before I was born, and who called me by his grace."
- Psalm 139:13–15 "You did form my inward parts, you knit me together in my mother's womb ... you knew me right well; my frame was not hidden from you, when I was being made in secret."

Abortion became legal in all nine months of pregnancy on January 22, 1973, with the Supreme Court decisions *Roe v. Wade* and *Doe v. Bolton*.

Norma McCorvey was the "Jane Roe" in the *Roe v. Wade* suit. She never had an abortion but filed her lawsuit while pregnant. While she was employed at an abortion clinic, she began to regret her lawsuit. Being interviewed 23 years later by *USA Today*, she stated that one evening, when no one else was there:

I went into the procedure room and laid down on the table ... trying to imagine what it would be like having an abortion ... I broke down and cried.

On *ABC's World News Tonight*, Norma McCorvey said: "I think abortion's wrong. I think what I did with *Roe v. Wade* was wrong."

• Proverbs 6 states: "The Lord hates ... hands that shed innocent blood."

• 2Kings 21 "Manasseh ... sacrificed his own son in the fire ... The Lord said ... 'Manasseh king of Judah has committed these detestable sins ... Therefore ... I am going to bring such disaster' ... Manasseh also shed so much innocent blood that he filled Jerusalem from end to end."

• 2 Chronicles 33:33 "Manasseh ... did that which was evil in the sight of the Lord, like unto the abominations of the heathen, whom the Lord had cast out before the children of Israel."

• Leviticus 20 "Anyone ... who sacrifices his child as a burnt offering to Molech ... I myself will turn against that man ... And if the people of the land pretend they do not know what the man has done ... then I myself will set my face against that man and his family."

• Proverbs 24:11–12 "Rescue those who are unjustly sentenced to death; don't stand back and let them die. Don't try to disclaim responsibility by saying you didn't know about it."

When Cain killed Abel, the Lord asked him:

"What hast thou done? the voice of thy brother's blood crieth unto me from the ground."

If the blood of one innocent person, Abel, cries out for judgment, how deafening is the cry from 60 million innocent unborn babies killed in the United States since 1973, in addition to an estimated one billion abortions globally?

Populations of western countries are declining, due, in part, to the attitude of Planned Parenthood's founder, Margaret Sanger, who wrote in *Woman and the New Race* (chapter 5, "The Wickedness of Creating Large Families," 1920):

> The most merciful thing that a large family does to one of its infant members is to kill it.

Sanger stated: "No woman shall have the legal right to bear a child ... without a permit." Former Senator Zel Miller stated in 2007:

> Here is the brutal truth that no one dares to mention: We're too few because too many of our babies have been killed. Over 45 millions since *Roe v. Wade* in 1973 ... It is not a proper fate for a human being made in God's image.

The largest ethnic group affected by abortion are African-Americans, as nearly 20 million black babies have been aborted since *Roe v. Wade*. A sign held up at the March for Life read: "Black Lives Matter – Even in the Womb."

Alveda King, niece of civil rights leader Rev. Martin Luther King, Jr., founded the National Black Pro-Life Coalition. She told CNSNews.com (Dec. 5, 2016):

> Abortion is ... designed for population control ... The numbers are higher in the African American community, so that's certainly black genocide ... We also discovered that once black people are made aware of the genocidal eugenics by abortion that the community will speak out.

The founder of Planned Parenthood, Margaret Sanger stated:

• The purpose of the American Baby Code shall be to provide for a better distribution of babies ... and to protect society against the propagation and increase of the unfit.

• Feeble minded persons ... and others found biologically unfit by authorities ... should be sterilized or, in cases of doubt, should be so isolated as to prevent the perpetuation of their afflictions by breeding.

• Knowledge of birth control is essentially moral. Its general, though prudent, practice must lead to a higher individuality and ultimately to a cleaner race. ("Morality and Birth Control", February–March, 1918, pp. 11,14.)

Sanger was quoted in "Apostle of Birth Control Sees Cause Gaining Here" (*The New York Times*, April 8, 1923, p. XII):

Birth control is ... cultivation of the better racial elements in our society, and the gradual suppression, elimination and eventual extirpation of defective stocks — those human weeds which threaten the blooming of the finest flowers of American civilization.

As cited in her *Autobiography*, (1938), Sanger told a KKK group in 1926:

Always to me any aroused group was a good group and therefore I accepted an invitation to talk to the women's branch of the Ku Klux Klan at Silver Lake, New

Jersey, one of the weirdest experiences I had in lecturing.

She stated in a radio interview on WFAB Syracuse, February 2, 1924 ("The Meaning of Radio Birth Control," April 1924, p. 111):

> Just think for a moment of the meaning of the word kindergarten — a garden of children ... In this matter we should not do less than follow the example of the professional gardener.

> Every expert gardener knows that the individual plant must be properly spaced, rooted in a rich nourishing soil, and provided with sufficient air and sunlight. He knows that no plant would have a fair chance of life if it were overcrowded or choked by weeds ...

> If plants, and livestock as well, require space and air, sunlight and love, children need them even more ... A farmer would rather produce a thousand thoroughbreds than a million runts. How are we to breed a race of human thoroughbreds unless we follow the same plan? We must make this country into a garden of children instead of a disorderly back lot overrun with human weeds.

Margaret Sanger's address to the New History Society, New York City, January 1, 1932, was summarized in "A Plan for Peace," April 1932, pp. 107–108:

> Keep the doors of immigration closed to the entrance of certain aliens whose condition is known to be detrimental to the stamina of the race, such as feeble-minded, idiots, morons, insane, syphilitic, epileptic ... and others in this class barred

by the immigration laws of 1924 ...

Apply a stern and rigid policy of sterilization and segregation to that grade of population whose progeny is tainted, or whose inheritance is such that objectionable traits may be transmitted to offspring ...

Insure the country against future burdens of maintenance for numerous offspring as may be born of feeble-minded parents, by pensioning all persons with transmissible disease who voluntarily consent to sterilization ... Give certain dysgenic groups in our population their choice of segregation or sterilization.

Sanger stated in *Pivot of Civilization* (1922, chapter 12, "Woman and the Future"):

We are informed that the psychological examination of the drafted men indicated that nearly half – 47.3 percent – of the population had the mentality of twelve-year-old children or less – in other words that they are morons ...

Our "overhead" expense in segregating the delinquent, the defective and the dependent, in prisons, asylums and permanent homes, our failure to segregate morons who are increasing and multiplying ... demonstrate our foolhardy and extravagant sentimentalism.

No industrial corporation could maintain its existence upon such a foundation. Yet hardheaded "captains of industry," financiers who pride themselves upon their cool-headed and keen-sighted business ability are dropping millions into rosewater philanthropies and charities that are silly at best and vicious at worst.

Supreme Court Justice Clarence Thomas wrote in his concurring opinion of *Box v. Planned Parenthood of Indiana and Kentucky*, May 28, 2019:

> In a report titled "Birth Control and the Negro," Sanger and her coauthors identified blacks as "the great problem of the South" — "the group with "the greatest economic, health, and social problems" — and developed a birth-control program geared toward this population.

> She later emphasized that black ministers should be involved in the program, noting, "We do not want word to go out that we want to exterminate the Negro population, and the minister is the man who can straighten out that idea if it ever occurs to any of their more rebellious members."

Justice Thomas continued:

> Some black groups saw "family planning as a euphemism for race genocide" and believed that black people were taking the brunt of the "planning" under Planned Parenthood's "ghetto approach" to distributing its services.

> "The Pittsburgh branch of the National Association for the Advancement of Colored People," for example, "criticized family planners as bent on trying to keep the Negro birth rate as low as possible" ...

> These observations echo the views articulated by the eugenicists and by Sanger decades earlier: "Birth Control of itself ... will make a better race" and tend "toward the elimination of the unfit."

Margaret Sanger's *Birth Control Review* (April 1933) published an article by Nazi advisor Ernst Rudin, one of the "fathers of racial hygiene," who wanted to eliminate inferior mankind – "untermensch."

Hippocrates of Kos (c.460–370 BC) is referred to as the "Father of Medicine" for starting the disciplined Hippocratic School of Medicine in the 4th century BC Greece. His attitude, "first, do no harm," was summed up in his work *Of the Epidemics*, Book I (c.400 BC):

Practice two things in your dealings with disease: either help or do not harm the patient.

He is credited with formulating "The Hippocratic Oath," which from ancient times, was taken by all medical practitioners:

I swear ... I will use those dietary regimens which will benefit my patients according to my greatest ability and judgment, and I will do no harm or injustice to them. I will not give a lethal drug to anyone if I am asked, nor will I advise such a plan; and similarly I will not give a woman a pessary to cause an abortion. In purity and according to divine law will I carry out my life and my art.

President Reagan addressed the March for Life, January 22, 1985:

I'm convinced, as I know you are, that our response to the 12th anniversary of *Roe v. Wade* and *Doe v. Bolton* must be to rededicate ourselves to ending the terrible national tragedy of abortion.

President Donald J. Trump addressed the thousands who gathered for the annual March for Life, January 20, 2018:

> The March for Life is a movement born out of love ... You love every child, born and unborn, because you believe that every life is sacred, that every child is a precious gift from God. We know that life is the greatest miracle of all. We see it in the eyes of every new mother who cradles that wonderful, innocent, and glorious newborn child in her loving arms ...
>
> Because of you, tens of thousands of Americans have been born and reached their full, God-given potential – because of you. As you all know, Roe vs. Wade has resulted in some of the most permissive abortion laws anywhere in the world ...
>
> The United States, it's one of only seven countries to allow elective late-term abortions, along with China, North Korea, and others. Right now, in a number of states, the laws allow a baby to be torn from his or her mother's womb in the ninth month. It is wrong; it has to change.

One of the many presentations changing views is the short video, 180 Movie, produced by Ray Comfort of New Zealand. Within seconds of viewing the film, people change from being pro-abortion to pro-life.

Gary Bauer wrote in the article "Pro-life is pro-science (*Washington Examiner*, 1/18/19):

> Every few months brings a technological advancement or scientific breakthrough

SANCTITY OF LIFE "SCIENTIFICALLY CORRECT ... LIFE BEGINS AT CONCEPTION"

that more fully reveals the unborn child as a living, feeling human being. Most of what we now know about the fetus was unknown or in dispute when *Roe* was decided in 1973 ...

We now know that at the moment of fertilization, a new, unique human embryo with unique DNA is created. We now know that even at that early stage, an individual human life exists. We now know that the unborn baby's heart begins to beat at three weeks, that brain waves can be detected as early as five weeks, and that all of the unborn baby's organs are fully formed by 24 weeks ...

We also know that unborn babies can feel pain at a point in the pregnancy when the most gruesome abortion procedures are still legal ... Science has exposed the lie that a first-trimester baby is merely a clump of cells or a blob of tissue — or anything other than a human being.

As Harvard Medical School's Micheline Matthews-Roth has put it: "It is scientifically correct to say that an individual human life begins at conception, when egg and sperm join to form the zygote, and this developing human always is a member of our species in all stages of its life."

President Trump continued his address to the March for Life, January 20, 2018:

Americans are more and more pro-life. You see that all the time. In fact, only 12 percent of Americans support abortion on demand at any time. Under my administration, we will always defend the very first right in the Declaration of Independence, and that is

AND THE FAITH OF THOSE WHO ACHIEVED THEM - WILLIAM J. FEDERER   243

the right to life ...

During my first week in office, I reinstated a policy first put in place by President Ronald Reagan, the Mexico City policy. I strongly supported the House of Representative's Pain-Capable bill, which would end painful, late-term abortions nationwide ... I call upon the Senate to pass this important law and send it to my desk for signing ...

Trump concluded:

Today, I'm announcing that we have just issued a new proposal to protect conscience rights and religious freedoms of doctors, nurses, and other medical professionals. So important.

I have also just reversed the previous administration's policy that restricted states' efforts to direct Medicaid funding away from abortion facilities that violate the law. We are protecting the sanctity of life and the family as the foundation of our society ...

That is why we march. That is why we pray. And that is why we declare that America's future will be filled with goodness, peace, joy, dignity, and life for every child of God.

Mother Teresa of Calcutta stated at the National Prayer Breakfast in Washington, D.C.,

February 3, 1994, with Bill and Hillary Clinton in attendance:

> The greatest destroyer of peace today is abortion, because it is a war against the child, a direct killing of the innocent child, murder by the mother herself, and if we accept that a mother can kill even her own child, how can we tell other people not to kill one another?

• Exodus 20:13 "Thou shalt not commit murder."

Mother Teresa added:

> Any country that accepts abortion is not teaching its people to love, but to use violence to get what they want. That is why the greatest destroyer of love and peace is abortion ...

> Many people are also concerned about all the violence in this great country of the United States ... But often these same people are not concerned with the millions who are being killed by the deliberate decision of their own mothers ...

> Jesus said, "Anyone who receives a child in my name, receives me" ... By aborting a child, a couple refuses to receive Jesus. Please don't kill the child ... Give me the child. I am willing ... to give that child to a married couple who will love the child and be loved by the child ...

From our children's home in Calcutta alone, we have saved over 3,000 children from abortion ... America can become a sign of peace ...

Mother Teresa concluded:

From here, a sign of care for the weakest of the weak – the unborn child – must go out to the world ... then really you will be true to what the founders of this country stood for.

The greatness of a nation is in how it treats its weakest members: the elderly, the infirm, the handicapped, the underprivileged, the unborn.

Ronald Reagan wrote in his article, "Abortion and the Conscience of the Nation," The *Human Life Review*, 1983:

Lincoln recognized that we could not survive as a free land when some men could decide that others were not fit to be free and should be slaves ... Likewise, we cannot survive as a free nation when some men decide that others are not fit to live and should be abandoned to abortion.

America's founders cared about their "children's children," called "posterity."

The Preamble of the U.S. Constitution, 1787, states:

We the people of the United States, in order to ... secure the blessings of liberty to ourselves and our posterity, do ordain and establish this Constitution.

If the Constitution is to "secure the blessings of liberty" to "our posterity," then the unborn need to be protected.

•Proverbs 13:22 states: "A good man leaves an inheritance to his children's children."

Ambassador Alan Keyes stated in a Virginia high school assembly, February 28, 2000:

How does it secure the blessings of liberty to our posterity, to those generations yet unborn, to kill them, aborting them in the womb?

Sir William Blackstone stated: "where life can be shown to exist, legal personhood exists." Those who fought in the Revolution were willing to sacrifice their prosperity for their posterity, pledging their lives and their fortunes.

Colonel William Prescott who fought at the Battle of Bunker Hill, stated August, 1774:

Our forefathers passed the vast Atlantic, spent their blood and treasure, that they might enjoy their liberties, both civil and religious, and transmit them to their posterity ... Now if we should give them up, can our children rise up and call us blessed?

Dr. Joseph Warren, who died in the Battle of Bunker Hill, wrote in the Suffolk Resolves, September of 1774:

That it is an indispensable duty which we owe to God, our country, ourselves and posterity ... to maintain, defend and preserve those civil and religious rights and liberties, for which many of our fathers fought, bled and died, and to hand them down entire to future generations.

Theodore Roosevelt stated March 4, 1905:

> If we fail, the cause of free self-government throughout the world will rock to its foundations, and therefore our responsibility is heavy, to ourselves, to the world as it is today, and to the generations yet unborn.

George Washington wrote in his Orders, July 2, 1776:

> The fate of unborn millions will now depend, under God, on the courage and conduct of this army ... We have, therefore to resolve to conquer or die.

On February 27, 2019, citizens of Toledo, Ohio, voted to grant "personhood" to Lake Erie:

> (UPI) "Voters in Toledo, Ohio, have become the first in the nation to grant a lake the same rights as a human being."

On January 14, 1988, Reagan asked that "personhood" be recognized for the unborn:

> The well-being and future of our country demand that protection of the innocents must be guaranteed and that the personhood of the unborn be declared and defended throughout our land.

• Psalm 127:3: "Lo, children are an heritage of the Lord: and the fruit of the womb is His reward."

CHEMIST CHAIM WEIZMANN & THE BIRTH OF MODERN ISRAEL

W hen World War I, it was not expected to last long. As the war continued, Britain's war effort was hindered by their ineffective manufacturing of explosives needed for ammunition.

The situation changed when a Jewish biochemist named Chaim Weizmann made a breakthrough in synthesizing the needed solvent, ethanol-butanol-acetone, by using a bacterial fermentation process. This revolutionized Britain's arms production.

Dr. Chaim Weizmann was born in Russia, November 27, 1874. His Jewish family had immigrated from Russia after Tsar's Alexander III's anti-Jewish pogroms of 1881–1884, the stories of which were the basis for the famous musical Fiddler on the Roof.

In gratitude for Dr. Chaim Weizmann's significant contributions to the nation's military, Britain's Foreign Secretary Lord Arthur Balfour issued the Balfour Declaration, November 2, 1917, establishing a home for Jews in the former Turkish land now under British control.

In his autobiography, *Trial and Error* (1949), Dr. Weizmann recounted his response to Lord Balfour's initial offer of giving Jews the British controlled country of Uganda:

"Mr. Balfour, supposing I was to offer you Paris instead of London, would you take it?" He sat up, looked at me, and answered: "But Dr. Weizmann, we have London." "That is true," I said, "but we had Jerusalem when London was a marsh."

He ... said two things which I remember vividly. The first was: "Are there many Jews who think like you?" I answered: "I believe I speak the mind of millions of Jews whom you will never see and who cannot speak for themselves" ... To this he said: "If that is so you will one day be a force."

British Prime Minister Lloyd-George had met with Chaim Weizmann in 1916, writing in his War Memoirs:

(Weizmann) explained his aspirations as to the repatriation of the Jews to the sacred land they had made famous. That was the fount and origin of the famous declaration about the National Home for the Jews in Palestine ... As soon as I became Prime Minister I talked the whole matter over with Mr Balfour, who was then Foreign Secretary.

The Balfour Declaration gave an area called the British Mandate to the Jews, stretching from Lebanon and Syria in the North; to Egypt and Arabia in the South; from the Mediterranean in the East; to Iraq in the West. The inspiration for Jews, who had been quietly resettling in their homeland for decades, came from Theodore Herzl's Zionist movement.

The Zionist movement initially grew out of America's 19th century Second Great Awakening Religious Revival where some evangelical Christians preached millennialism, and that Jewish resettlement was necessary before the coming of Christ and the Advent of the Millennium Kingdom.

Anita Shapira wrote in *Israel a History* (Weidenfeld & Nicolson, 2014, p15):

> The idea of the Jews returning to their ancient homeland as the first step to world redemption seems to have originated among a specific group of evangelical English Protestants that flourished in England in the 1840s; they passed this notion onto Jewish circles.

Geoffrey Alderman wrote in the *Jewish Chronicle,* November 8, 2012:

> The Balfour Declaration was born out of religious sentiment. Arthur Balfour was a Christian mystic who believed that the Almighty had chosen him to be an instrument of the Divine Will, the purpose of which was to restore the Jews to their ancient homeland — perhaps as a precursor to the Second Coming of the Messiah.
>
> The Declaration was thus intended to assist in the fulfillment of biblical prophecy. This appealed to Lloyd George, whose private immorality did not prevent him from believing in the prophecies of a Bible he knew inside out.

Anti-semitism and persecution of Jews increased in Eastern Europe and Russia in the 1800s. This contributed to Jewish leaders becoming convinced that the only safe haven for the Jews was to have their own state.

Britain's promise during World War I was, that if Jews worldwide, particularly in America, would politically and financially support Britain against the German–Ottoman

Alliance, then after the war, Britain would support a Jewish state carved out of the defeated Ottoman Empire.

Lord Balfour addressed a Jewish gathering, February 7,1918:

My personal hope is that the Jews will make good in Palestine and eventually found a Jewish state. It is up to them now; we have given them their great opportunity.

In 1919, Lord Balfour wrote to Lord George Curzon:

In Palestine we do not propose even to go through the form of consulting the wishes of the present inhabitants of the country ... The Four Great Powers are committed to Zionism. And Zionism, be it right or wrong, good or bad, is rooted in age-long traditions, in present needs, in future hopes, of far profounder import than the desires and prejudices of the 700,000 Arabs who now inhabit that ancient land.

Democrat President Truman wrote to Israel's President Dr. Chaim Weizmann, November 29, 1948:

I have interpreted my re-election as a mandate ... to carry out ... the plank on Israel ... In closing, I want to tell you how happy and impressed I have been at the remarkable progress made by the new State of Israel.

Dr. Chaim Weizmann had stated:

I think that the God of Israel is with us.

℞

ALBERT EINSTEIN
"I OBSERVE THE LAWS OF NATURE..."

Albert Einstein was born in Germany on March 14, 1879. He began teaching himself calculus at age 14.

While a student at physics–mathematics section of the Polytechnic Institute in Zurich, he met Mileva Marić, whom he studied together with. She helped him with papers and articles, advancing his career. They eventually married in 1903. Albert and Mileva had a daughter, Lieserl, and two sons, Hans Albert and Eduard.

Correspondence indicates she may have contributed materially to his early research, so much so, that after their divorce in 1919, he gave her the money from winning the Nobel Prize.

With a doctorate from the University of Zurich, Einstein wrote papers on electromagnetic energy, relativity, and statistical mechanics. He predicted a ray of light from a distant star would appear to bend as it passed near the Sun. When an eclipse confirmed this, *The London Times* ran the headline, November 7, 1919, "Revolution in science – New theory of the Universe – Newtonian ideas overthrown."

In 1921, he was awarded the Nobel Prize in physics. The periodic table's 99th element was named "einsteinium" in 1955 after his death.

His first visit to the United States was to raise funds for Jerusalem's Hebrew University. On his 3rd visit, 1932, he took a post at Princeton University. Princeton's Fine Hall has his words inscribed above the fireplace:

Raffiniert ist der Herr Gott, aber Boshaft ist er nicht. (God is clever, but not dishonest,)

Paraphrasing Miguel de Cervantes' quote "I do not believe that the Good Lord plays dice," Einstein said: "God Almighty does not throw dice," and added: "Before God we are all equally wise – equally foolish."

He married his cousin, Elsa, in 1921 and they lived together till her death in 1936. His accountant, Leo Mattersdorf of New York, wrote (*TIME Magazine*, 1963):

One year while I was at his Princeton home preparing his return, Mrs. Elsa Einstein, who was then still living, asked me to stay for lunch. During the course of the meal, the professor (Einstein) turned to me and with his inimitable chuckle said: "The hardest thing in the world to understand is income taxes."

Einstein stayed in the United States, becoming a citizen in 1940. When the National Socialist Workers Party (Nazi) took control of Germany, they barred Jews from holding official positions. Anti-semitism on university campuses forbade Jews teaching. Nazi propaganda minister Joseph Goebbels declared "Jewish intellectualism is dead" and burned books by Jewish authors, including Einstein's works. Jewish poet Heinrich Heine prophetically penned in 1822: "Where they burn books, they will, in the end, burn human beings too."

Einstein's warning that Nazis could create the atom bomb led President Franklin

Roosevelt to set up the Manhattan Project. His theory of relativity, E=MC2, is the basis for applying atomic energy. He humorously described relativity:

When a man sits with a pretty girl for an hour, it seems like a minute. But let him sit on a hot stove for a minute – and it's longer than any hour. That's relativity.

Commenting on socialist redistribution of wealth, Albert Einstein stated:

I am absolutely convinced that no wealth in the world can help humanity forward, even in the hands of the most devoted worker in this cause. The example of great and pure individuals is the only thing that can lead us to noble thoughts and deeds ... Can anyone imagine Moses, Jesus, or Gandhi armed with the moneybags of Carnegie?

In November of 1952, Prime Minister David Ben-Gurion asked Einstein to be Israel's 2nd President, but he declined due to age, dying less than 3 years later. Being "deeply moved" by the offer, Einstein replied:

My relationship with the Jewish people became my strongest human tie.

Einstein was quoted in *The New York Times*, November 9, 1930:

I assert that the cosmic religious experience is the strongest and noblest driving force behind scientific research.

As recorded by Helen Dukas in *Albert Einstein, The Human Side* (Princeton University Press, 1981, p. 66), Einstein stated:

My religiosity consists in a humble admiration of the infinitely superior spirit that reveals itself in the little that we, with our weak and transitory understanding, can comprehend of reality. Morality is of the highest importance – but for us, not for God.

He stated in an interview published in G.S. Viereck's book *Glimpses of the Great*, 1930:

> I'm absolutely not an atheist ... The problem involved is too vast for our limited minds. We are in the position of a little child entering a huge library filled with books in many languages. The child knows someone must have written those books. It does not know how. It does not understand the languages in which they are written.
>
> The child dimly suspects a mysterious order in the arrangement of the books but doesn't know what it is. That, it seems to me, is the attitude of even the most intelligent human being toward God. We see the universe marvelously arranged and obeying certain laws but only dimly understand these laws.

Walter Isaacson quoted Einstein in "Einstein and Faith," *Time* 169, April 5, 2007, 47):

> The fanatical atheists ... are like slaves who are still feeling the weight of their chains which they have thrown off after hard struggle. They are creatures who – in their grudge against the traditional "opium of the people" – cannot bear the "music of the spheres."

According to Prince Hubertus (Ronald Clark, *Einstein: The Life and Times*, NY: World Pub. Co. 1971, p. 425), Einstein stated:

> In view of such harmony in the cosmos which I, with my limited human mind, am able to recognize, there are yet people who say there is no God. But what really makes me angry is that they quote me for the support of such views.

Einstein's reference to the "music of the spheres" is a religious concept used from the Scientific Revolution to describe an orbital resonance of the planets. Johannes Kepler, who discovered the laws of planetary motion, wrote in *The Harmonies of the World*, 1619:

> Holy Father, keep us safe in the concord of our love for one another, that we may be one just as Thou art with Thy Son, Our Lord, and with the Holy Ghost, and just as through the sweetest bonds of harmonies Thou hast made all Thy works one, and that from the bringing of Thy people into concord, the body of Thy Church may be built up in the Earth, as Thou didst erect the heavens themselves out of harmonies.

Yale professor Benjamin Silliman, who founded the *American Journal of Science and Arts* in 1818, similarly stated:

> The relation of geology, as well as astronomy, to the Bible, when both are well understood, is that of perfect harmony ... The Word and the works of God cannot

conflict, and the more they are studied the more perfect will their harmony appear.

In 1931, astronomer Edwin Hubble invited Albert Einstein to the Mount Wilson Observatory in Pasadena, California. After viewing the "red shift" of distant stars revealing an expanding universe, Einstein remarked "I now see the necessity of a beginning."

In *Einstein and the Poet: In Search of the Cosmic Man* (1983), William Hermanns recorded Einstein's 1943 statement:

Creation may be spiritual in origin, but that doesn't mean that everything created is spiritual ... Let us accept the world is a mystery. Nature is neither solely material nor entirely spiritual. Man, too, is more than flesh and blood; otherwise, no religions would have been possible.

Behind each cause is still another cause ... Yet, only one thing must be remembered: there is no effect without a cause, and there is no lawlessness in creation.

Einstein wrote to M. Berkowitz, 1950, (William Hermanns, *Einstein and the Poet. In Search of the Cosmic Man*, Brookline Village MA: Branden Books, 1983, p. 60):

"God" is a mystery ... I have nothing but awe when I observe the laws of nature. There are not laws without a lawgiver, but how does this lawgiver look?

Though not believing in a personal God, *The Saturday Evening Post*, October 26, 1929, published George Sylvester Viereck's interview with Einstein, in which he stated:

As a child I received instruction both in the Bible and in the Talmud. I am a Jew, but I am enthralled by the luminous figure of the Nazarene ... Emil Ludwig's (book on) Jesus is shallow. Jesus is too colossal for the pen of phrasemongers, however artful. No man can dispose of Christianity with a bon mot! (witty remark). No one can read the Gospels without feeling the actual presence of Jesus. His personality pulsates in every word. No myth is filled with such life.

ପ୍ଲ

ROBERT GODDARD
"FATHER OF MODERN ROCKETRY"

The "Father of Modern Rocketry" was American scientist Robert H. Goddard. He ushered in the "Space Age" by creating the world's first liquid-fueled rocket.

Goddard was born in 1882 and raised Episcopalian. He wrote of a pivotal moment when he was 17-years-old, after having read H.G. Wells' 1897 science-fiction novel *War of the Worlds:*

On the afternoon of October 19, 1899, I climbed a tall cherry tree and, armed with a saw which I still have, and a hatchet, started to trim the dead limbs from the cherry tree.

It was one of the quiet, colorful afternoons of sheer beauty which we have in October in New England, and as I looked towards ... the east, I imagined how wonderful it would be to make some device which had even the possibility of ascending to Mars. I was a different boy when I descended the tree from when I ascended for existence at last seemed very purposive ...

He continued:

The dream would not down ... for even though I reasoned with myself that the thing was impossible, there was something inside which simply would not stop working.

In 1919, he published a ground-breaking work titled "A Method of Reaching Extreme Altitudes," where a rocket would be guided by a gyroscope connected to steerable thrust to provide three-axis control. In 1924, he married Esther Christine Kisk at St. John's Episcopal Church in Worcester, Massachusetts. She faithfully assisted him as his secretary, recording his research and applying for patents.

Goddard's team launched 34 different rockets between 1926 and 1941, setting records of 550 miles an hour and an altitude of 1.6 miles. He received funding from Charles Lindbergh and the Guggenheim family.

The press ridiculed him, as Reagan explained to the National Space Club, March 29, 1985:

In Dr. Goddard's case, *The New York Times* claiming rockets would never work in the vacuum of space ridiculed his effort. "He only seems to lack the knowledge ladled out daily in high schools," the *Times* editorialized.

Only after the successful launch of Apollo 11, decades after Goddard's death, did *The New York Times* published a short correction, July 17, 1969:

Further investigation and experimentation have confirmed ... that a rocket can function in a vacuum as well as in an atmosphere. The *Times* regrets the error.

After his death in 1945, appreciation for Goddard's work increased so much so that NASA named the Goddard Space Flight Center after him in 1959. He was posthumously inducted into the International Aerospace Hall of Fame, 1966, and the International Space Hall of Fame, 1976. Robert Goddard stated:

• Every vision is a joke until the first man accomplishes it; once realized, it becomes commonplace.

• It is difficult to say what is impossible, for the dream of yesterday is the hope of today and the reality of tomorrow.

• Set goals, challenge yourself, and achieve them. Live a healthy life ... and make every moment count. Rise above the obstacles, and focus on the positive.

President Reagan continued his address to the National Space Club, March 29, 1985:

Personally, I like space. The higher you go, the smaller the Federal Government looks ... Robert Goddard, our American rocket pioneer ... exemplified the ingenuity, the perseverance of individuals who make lasting contributions to their fellow countrymen and to mankind. Dr. Goddard persevered for decades of intense research and development ...

Due to the efforts of Dr. Goddard and other individuals of vision and tenacity, America is now on the edge of a new era. By standing on the shoulders of giants like Robert Goddard, this generation is moving forward to harness the enormity of space in the preservation of peace ...

American freedom was once protected by musket and ball. Today scientific advancements are changing the way we think about our security ... If you'll pardon my stealing a film line: "The force is with us" ...

Reagan continued:

We have used and will continue to use space to make ours a safer world ... Space technology has already revolutionized communications and is assisting everyone from farmers to navigators ...

Space, like freedom, is a limitless, never-ending frontier on which our citizens can prove that they are indeed Americans. Dr. Goddard once wrote a letter to H.G. Wells in which he explained: "There can be no thoughts of finishing, for aiming at the stars, both literally and figuratively, is a problem to occupy generations, so that no matter how much progress one makes, there is always the thrill of just beginning."

Well, let us hope that Americans never lose that thrill ... God bless you all.

Wernher von Braun stated:

 Don't you know about your own rocket pioneer? Dr. Goddard was ahead of us all.

Braun added:

Goddard's rockets ... may have been rather crude by present-day standards, but they blazed the trail and incorporated many features used in our most modern rockets and space vehicles.

After Robert Goddard successfully launched his first liquid-fueled rocket in 1926, news spread. Wernher von Braun read the newspaper reports and began corresponding with him. The next year, 1927, he started the German Rocket Society. That same year that Charles A. Lindbergh flew from New York to Paris. World relations with Germany had not yet become hostile.

In 1929, Lindbergh began supporting Goddard's work. In the 1930s, Lindbergh was sent by the U.S. military to Germany to assess their aviation. While there, he was presented with the Service Cross of the German Eagle on behalf of Adolf Hitler.

In 1936, the Olympics were held in Berlin, where Hitler had built a 100,000 seat stadium. Not suspecting their ill-intent, Goddard naively answered telephone inquiries from German rocket engineers.

By 1939, Goddard ended this when he suspected his research was being co-opted by Germany's National Socialist Workers Party. In 1940, Goddard began warning officials in the U.S. Army and Navy of the growing Nazi rocket threat, although his warnings were largely ignored. The U.S. Army was not interested, but the U.S. Navy was.

From 1942, till his death in 1945, Goddard was director of research developing experimental engines at the U.S. Navy's Bureau of Aeronautics at Annapolis, Maryland.

CR

WERNHER VON BRAUN
"FATHER OF MODERN SPACE FLIGHT"

The "Father of Modern Space Flight." When World War II started, Wernher von Braun was a graduate student. In Nazi Germany, as on many campuses today, if a scientist refused to comply with the prevailing politically correct view, his or her career in academia was ended.

Braun was recruited by the National Socialist Workers Party to work as a scientist developing the V-2 rocket. The V2 rocket was the world's first long-range guided ballistic missile, and it wreaked devastating destruction on Allied cities, including London, Antwerp and Liège.

As the War neared its end, in May of 1945, the United States and the Union of Soviet Socialist Republics were racing against each other to capture the German scientists. Braun and the other Germany scientists decided to escape to the American side rather than the Soviet Union. Suffering a broken arm during his escape, he explained:

> I myself, and everybody you see here, have decided to go West. And I think our decision was not one of expediency, but a moral decision. We knew that we had created a new means of warfare, and the question as ... to what victorious nation we were willing to entrust this brainchild of ours was a moral decision more than

anything else ...

We wanted ... to see the world spared another conflict such as Germany had just been through, and we felt that only by surrendering such a weapon to people who are guided by the Bible could such an assurance to the world be best secured.

Braun emigrated to the United States where he became a U.S. citizen in 1955, calling it "one of the proudest and most significant days of my life." In 1958, he launched America's first satellite.

He worked on the U.S. guided missile program and was director of NASA's Marshall Space Flight Center. He was the chief architect of the Saturn V booster rocket, the most powerful rocket ever brought to operational status, being over a football field in length from top to base.

President John F. Kennedy stated at Rice University, September 12, 1962:

William Bradford, speaking in 1630 of the founding of the Plymouth Bay Colony, said that all great and honorable actions are accompanied with great difficulties, and both must be ... overcome with answerable courage.

Kennedy continued:

But if I were to say, my fellow citizens, that we shall send to the moon, 240,000 miles away from the control station in Houston, a giant rocket more than 300 feet tall, the length of this football field,

made of new metal alloys, some of which have not yet been invented, capable of standing heat and stresses several times more than have ever been experienced, fitted together with a precision better than the finest watch,

carrying all the equipment needed for propulsion, guidance, control, communications, food and survival, on an untried mission, to an unknown celestial body, and then return it safely to earth,

re-entering the atmosphere at speeds of over 25,000 miles per hour, causing heat about half that of the temperature of the sun ... and do all this, and do it right, and do it first before this decade is out – then we must be bold.

Space is there, and we're going to climb it, and the moon and the planets are there, and new hopes for knowledge and peace are there. And, therefore, as we set sail we ask God's blessing on the most hazardous and dangerous and greatest adventure on which man has ever embarked.

The Saturn V was the only launch vehicle powerful enough to lift beyond low Earth orbit a spacecraft capable of carrying humans. An Ares V rocket was designed to surpass the Saturn V, but President Obama canceled the Constellation Program in 2010. Advances in manned spaceflight have continued with innovative companies such as: SpaceX, Orbital, Blue Origin, Northrop Grumman, Boeing, and Sierra Nevada Corporation.

Braun received the National Medal of Science in 1975, and is considered "without doubt, the greatest rocket scientist in history." As founder of the National Space Institute, he stated:

> In this age of space flight, when we use the modern tools of science to advance into new regions of human activity, the Bible – this grandiose, stirring history of the gradual revelation and unfolding of the moral law – remains in every way an up-to-date book.
>
> Our knowledge and use of the laws of nature that enable us to fly to the Moon also enable us to destroy our home planet with the atom bomb. Science itself does not address the question whether we should use the power at our disposal for good or for evil.
>
> The guidelines of what we ought to do are furnished in the moral law of God ... It is no longer enough that we pray that God may be with us on our side. We must learn to pray that we may be on God's side."

Wernher von Braun wrote in *This Week Magazine,* January 1, 1961:

> But I can't help feeling at the same time that this space effort of ours is bigger even than a rivalry between the United States and Russia ... The heavens beyond us are enormous beyond comprehension, and the further we penetrate them, the greater will be our human understanding of the great universal purpose, the Divine Will itself.

Braun wrote to the California State Board of Education, September 14, 1972:

> Dear Mr. Grose: In response to your inquiry about my personal views concerning the "Case for DESIGN" as a viable scientific theory or the origin of the universe, life and man, I am pleased to make the following observations.

For me, the idea of a creation is not conceivable without evoking the necessity of design. One cannot be exposed to the law and order of the universe without concluding that there must be design and purpose behind it all. In the world round us, we can behold the obvious manifestations of an ordered, structured plan or design.

We can see the will of the species to live and propagate. And we are humbled by the powerful forces at work on a galactic scale, and the purposeful orderliness of nature that endows a tiny and ungainly seed with the ability to develop into a beautiful flower. The better we understand the intricacies of the universe and all harbors, the more reason we have found to marvel at the inherent design upon which it is based ...

Braun continued:

While the admission of a design for the universe ultimately raises the question of a Designer (a subject outside of science), the scientific method does not allow us to exclude data which lead to the conclusion that the universe, life and man are based on design.

To be forced to believe only one conclusion – that everything in the universe happened by chance – would violate the very objectivity of science itself. Certainly, there are those who argue that the universe evolved out of a random process, but what random process could produce the brain of a man or the system or the human eye? ...

He added:

Some people say that science has been unable to prove the existence of a Designer. They admit that many of the miracles in the world around us are hard to understand, and they do not deny that the universe, as modern science sees it, is indeed a far more wondrous thing than the creation medieval man could perceive.

But they still maintain that since science has provided us with so many answers the day will soon arrive when we will be able to understand even the creation of the fundamental laws of nature without a Divine intent.

They challenge science to prove the existence of God. But must we really light a candle to see the sun? Many men who are intelligent and of good faith say they cannot visualize a Designer. Well, can a physicist visualize an electron? The electron is materially inconceivable and yet it is so perfectly known through its effects that we use it to illuminate our cities, guide our airlines through the night skies and take the most accurate measurements ...

He stated further:

What strange rationale makes some physicists accept the inconceivable electrons as real while refusing to accept the reality of a Designer on the ground that they cannot conceive Him?

I am afraid that, although they really do not understand the electron either, they are ready to accept it because they managed to produce a rather clumsy mechanical model of it borrowed from rather limited experience in other fields, but they would not know how to begin building a model of God.

I have discussed the aspect of a Designer at some length because it might be that the primary resistance to acknowledging the "Case for Design" as a viable scientific alternative to the current "Case for Chance" lies in the inconceivability, in some scientists' minds, of a Designer.

The inconceivability of some ultimate issue (which will always lie outside scientific resolution) should not be allowed to rule out any theory that explains the interrelationship of observed data and is useful for prediction ...

Braun concluded:

We in NASA were often asked what the real reason was for the amazing string of successes we had with our Apollo flights to the Moon. I think the only honest answer we could give was that we tried to never overlook anything.

It is in that same sense of scientific honesty that I endorse the presentation of alternative theories for the origin of the universe, life and man in the science classroom. It would be an error to overlook the possibility that the universe was planned rather than happened by chance. With kindest regards. Sincerely, Wernher von Braun."

Wernher von Braun wrote an article titled "My Faith: A space-age scientist tells why he must believe in God" (*American Weekly*, February 10, 1963, Foreword to his *Anthology on the Creation and Design exhibited in Nature*):

The two most powerful forces shaping our civilization today are science and religion. Through science man strives to learn more of the mysteries of creation. Through religion he seeks to know the Creator. Neither operates independently.

It is as difficult for me to understand a scientist who does not acknowledge the presence of a superior rationality behind the existence of the universe as it is to comprehend a theologian who would deny the advances of science. Far from being independent or opposing forces, science and religion are sisters. Both seek a better world.

While science seeks control over the forces of nature around us, religion controls the forces of nature within us ...

He continued:

As we learn more and more about nature, we become more deeply impressed and humbled by its orderliness and unerring perfection. Our expanding knowledge of the laws of the universe have enabled us to send men out of their natural environment into the strange new environment of space, and return them safely to earth.

Since we first began the exploration of space through rocketry, we have regularly received letters expressing concern over what the writers call our "tampering" with God's creation. Some writers view with dismay the possibility of upsetting the delicate balance of the tremendous forces of nature that permit life on our globe ...

Braun added:

One letter revealed an honest fear that a rocket would strike an angel in space high above the earth. And one of the Russian cosmonauts stated flatly after his earth-circling flight in space: "I was looking around attentively all day during my flight, but I didn't find anybody there – neither angels nor God ..."

Such shallow thinking is childish and pathetic. I have no fear that a physical object will harm any spiritual entities. Manned space flight is an amazing achievement. But it has opened for us thus far only a tiny door for viewing the awesome reaches of space.

Our outlook through this peephole at the vast mysteries or the universe only confirms our belief in the certainty of its Creator. Finite man cannot comprehend an omnipresent, omniscient, omnipotent, and infinite God. Any effort to visualize God, to reduce him to our comprehension, to describe him in our language, beggars his greatness.

I find it best through faith to accept God as an Intelligent Will, perfect in goodness, revealing himself in the world of experience more fully down through the ages, as man's capacity for understanding grows. For spiritual comfort I find assurance in the concept of the fatherhood of God. For ethical guidance I rely on the corollary concept of the brotherhood of man ...

He stated further:

Scientists now believe that in nature, matter is never destroyed.

Not even the tiniest particle can disappear without a trace. Nature does not know extinction – only transformation. Would God have less regard for his masterpiece of creation, the human soul? Each person receives a gift of life on this earth.

A belief in the continuity of spiritual existence, after the comparative mere flick of three score and ten years of physical life here in the endless cycle of eternity, makes the action of each moment like an investment with far-reaching dividends. The knowledge that man can choose between good and evil should draw him closer to his Creator ...

Braun concluded:

Next, the realization should dawn that his survival here and hereafter depends on his adherence to the spiritual rather than the scientific. Our decisions undeniably influence the course of future events.

Nature around us still harbors more unsolved than solved mysteries. But science has mastered enough of these forces to usher in a golden age for all mankind, if this power is used for good – or to destroy us, if evil triumphs.

The ethical guidelines of religion are the bonds that can hold our civilization together. Without them man can never attain that cherished goal of lasting peace with himself, his God, and his fellowman.

Erik Bergaust's book, *Wernher von Braun: The authoritative and definitive biographical profile of the father of modern space flight* (National Space Institute, Washington, DC, 1976), quoted Wernher von Braun as stating:

The laws of creation and the divine intentions underlying the creation. Through science man attempts to understand the laws of creation; through religious activities he attempts to understand the intentions of the Creator. Each approach is a search for ultimate truth ...

There have been conflicts in the relationship between science and religion ... Personally, I find this state of affairs unsatisfactory, for I wish to regard the Creator and His creation as an entity ... science and religion are like two windows in a house through which we look at the reality of the Creator and the laws manifested in His creation.

As long as we see two different images through these two windows and cannot reconcile them, we must keep trying to obtain a more complete and better integrated total picture of the ultimate reality by properly tying together our scientific and religious concepts ...

He stated further:

The more we learn about God's creation, the more I am impressed with the orderliness and unerring perfection of the natural laws that govern it. In this perfection, man – the scientist – catches of glimpse of the Creator and His design for nature. The man-to-God relationship is deepened in the devout scientist as his knowledge of the natural laws grows.

Wernher von Braun died June 16, 1977. As Vice-President of Engineering and

Development at Fairchild Industries, he wrote the forward to Harold Hill's book *From Goo to You by Way of the Zoo* (Plainfield, NJ: Logos International, 1976):

Six Apollo crews have visited the moon and returned safely to earth. The Skylab astronauts have spent 171 days, 13 hours, and 14 minutes working and living in space, and all have returned hale and hearty to earth.

Why are we flying to the moon? What is our purpose? What is the essential justification for the exploration of space? The answer, I am convinced, lies rooted not in whimsy, but in the nature of man. Whereas all other living beings seem to find their places in the natural order and fulfill their role in life with a kind of calm acceptance, man clearly exhibits confusion.

Why the anxiety? Why the storm and stress? Man really seems to be the only living thing uncertain of his role in the universe; and in his uncertainty, he has been calling since time immemorial upon the stars and the heavens for salvation and for answers to his eternal questions: Who am I? Why am I here? ...

Astronomy is the oldest science, existed for thousands of years as the only science, and is today considered the queen of the sciences. Although man lacks the eye of the night owl, the scent of the fox, or the hearing of the deer, he has an uncanny ability to learn about abstruse things like the motions of the planets, the cradle-to-the-grave cycle of the stars, and the distance between stars.

The mainspring of science is curiosity. There have always been men and women who felt a burning desire to know what was under the rock, beyond the hills, across the oceans. This restless breed now wants to know what makes an atom work, through what process life reproduces itself, or what is the geological history of the moon.

But there would not be a single great accomplishment in the history of mankind without faith. Any man who strives to accomplish something needs a degree of faith. But many people find the churches, those old ramparts of faith, badly battered by the onslaught of three hundred years of scientific skepticism ...

Braun added:

This has led many to believe that science and religion are not compatible, that "knowing" and "believing" cannot live side by side. Nothing could be further from the truth. Science and religion are not antagonists. On the contrary, they are sisters.

While science tries to learn more about the creation, religion tries to better understand the Creator ... For me the idea of a creation is inconceivable without God. One cannot be exposed to the law and order of the universe without concluding that there must be a divine intent behind it all.

Some evolutionists believe that the creation is the result of a random arrangement

of atoms and molecules over billions of years. But when they consider the development of the human brain by random processes within a time span of less than a million years, they have to admit that this span is just not long enough. Or take the evolution of the eye in the animal world.

What random process could possibly explain the simultaneous evolution of the eye's optical system, the conductors of the optical signals from the eye to the brain, and the optical nerve center in the brain itself where the incoming light impulses are converted to an image the conscious mind can comprehend?

Our space ventures have been only the smallest of steps in the vast reaches of the universe and have introduced more mysteries than they have solved ...

He stated further:

Speaking for myself, I can only say that the grandeur of the cosmos serves to confirm my belief in the certainty of a Creator. Of course, the discoveries in astronomy, biology, physics, and even in psychology have shown that we have to enlarge the medieval image of God.

If there is a mind behind the immense complexities of the multitude of phenomena which man, through the tools of science, can now observe, then it is that of a Being tremendous in His power and wisdom.

But we should not be dismayed by the relative insignificance of our own planet in the vast universe as modern science now sees it. In fact God deliberately reduced Himself to the stature of humanity in order to visit the earth in person, because the cumulative effect over the centuries of millions of individuals choosing to please themselves rather than God had infected the whole planet.

When God became a man Himself, the experience proved to be nothing short of pure agony. In man's time-honored fashion, they would unleash the whole arsenal of weapons against Him: misrepresentation, slander, and accusation of treason ...

The stage was set for a situation without parallel in the history of the earth. God would visit creatures and they would nail Him to the cross! Although I know of no reference to Christ ever commenting on scientific work, I do know that He said, "Ye shall know the truth, and the truth shall make you free."

Thus I am certain that, were He among us today, Christ would encourage scientific research as modern man's most noble striving to comprehend and admire His Father's handiwork. The universe as revealed through scientific inquiry is the living witness that God has indeed been at work.

Wernher von Braun concluded:

When astronaut Frank Borman returned from his unforgettable Christmas, 1968, flight around the moon with Apollo 8, he was told that a Soviet Cosmonaut recently returned from a space flight had commented that he had seen neither God nor angels on his flight. Had Borman seen God? the reporter inquired. Frank Borman replied, "No, I did not see Him either, but I saw His evidence."